SIDMOUTH

YESTERDAY'S SHOPS

Compiled by
John Ankins with my Daughter Margaret

Typesetting by A & P Tully, S. W. Typesetting, Sidmouth

Printed by Westprint,
Clyst Court, Hill Barton Business Park, Clyst St. Mary, Exeter EX5 1SA

First Published in November 1999 by J. Ankins

Second Edition revised and updated December 2001

© Copyright J. Ankins

ISBN 0-9538021-0-8

CONTENTS

Introduction	1
All Saints Road	132
Church Street, South Side	122
Church Street, North Side	127
East Street	134
Fore Street, East Side	65
Fore Street, West Side	85
High Street, East Side	27
High Street, West Side	49
Holmdale	136
Market Place	113
Mill Street	139
New Street	94
Old Fore Street, East Side	101
Old Fore Street, West Side	108
Prospect Place	116
Radway Place	23
Russell Street	148
Temple Street, East Side	5
Temple Street, West Side	15
Vicarage Road	22
REFERENCES	150
MAP	iii

Glossary of Numbered Sites

① Potburys
② Temple Gardens
③ Volunteer
④ Site of Brewery
⑤ Police Station
⑥ Apollonia House
⑦ Old Post Office
⑧ Radway Cinema
⑨ Conservative Club
⑩ Unitarian Chapel
⑪ Radway Inn
⑫ Fords
⑬ Old Fire Station
⑭ Shopping Centre
⑮ Somerfield
⑯ Thatched House
⑰ Natwest Bank
⑱ Site Grand Cinema
⑲ Lloyds Bank
⑳ Potburys

㉑ Woolworths
㉒ Anchor Inn
㉓ Museum
㉔ Gliddons Toys
㉕ Gliddons Ironmongers
㉖ Fields
㉗ Marlborough
㉘ Mocha
㉙ Cards for all Seasons
㉚ Market Building
㉛ Mountstephen
㉜ The Dove Inn
㉝ HSBC Bank (Midland)
㉞ York Hotel
㉟ Libra Court
㊱ Knights
㊲ Roxburgh
㊳ Red Cross HQ
㊴ Ford over River

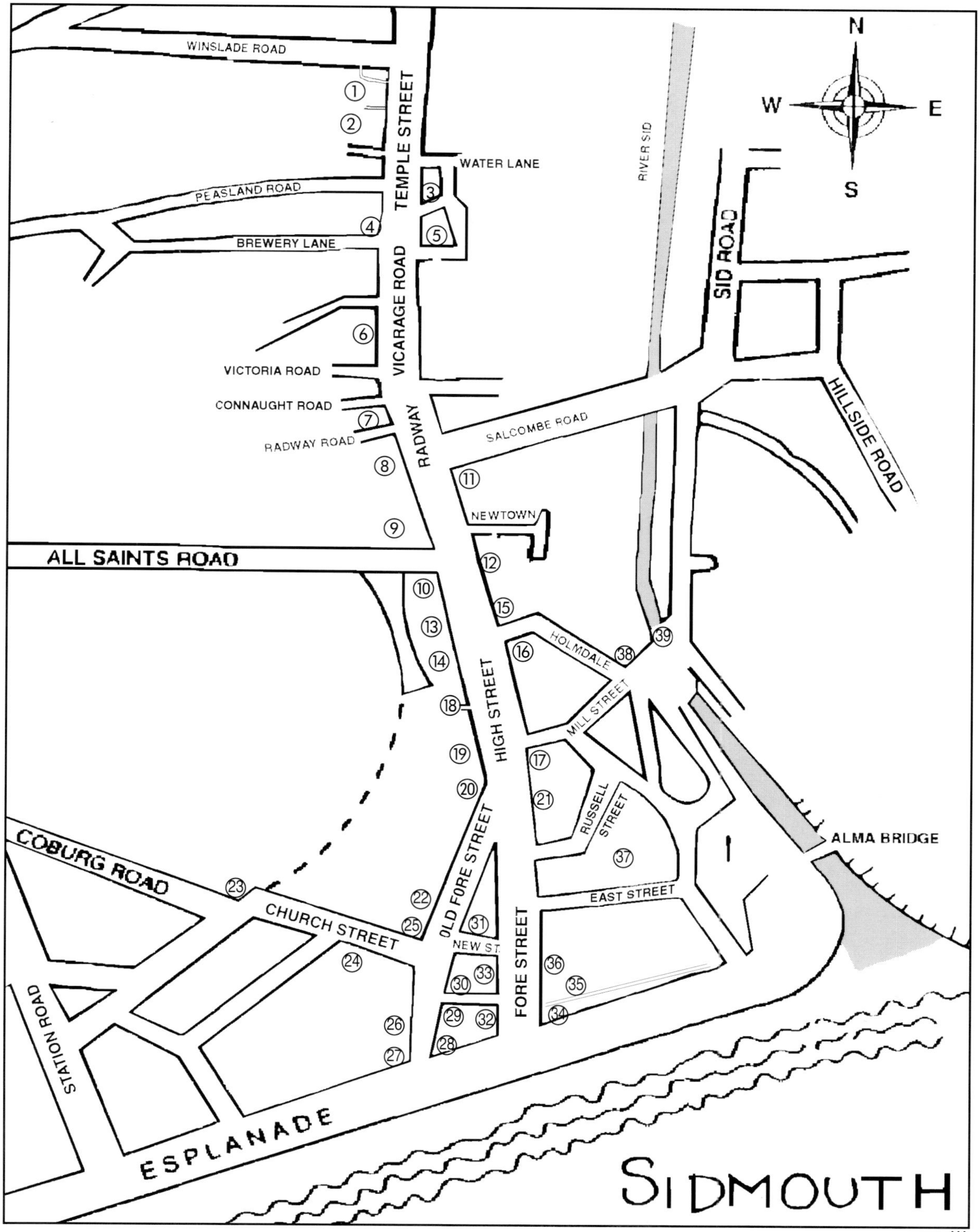
N
W
E
S
WINSLADE ROAD
TEMPLE STREET
WATER LANE
RIVER SID
PEASLAND ROAD
BREWERY LANE
SID ROAD
VICARAGE ROAD
VICTORIA ROAD
CONNAUGHT ROAD
RADWAY ROAD
RADWAY
SALCOMBE ROAD
HILLSIDE ROAD
NEWTOWN
ALL SAINTS ROAD
HOLMDALE
HIGH STREET
MILL STREET
RUSSELL STREET
ALMA BRIDGE
COBURG ROAD
OLD FORE STREET
EAST STREET
CHURCH STREET
NEW ST.
FORE STREET
STATION ROAD
ESPLANADE
SIDMOUTH

PHOTOGRAPHS

Baker, Temple Street	6
Bell and Posta Shops	34
Biffen, High Street	49
Binocular Shop, Old Fore Street	101
Bovett, Fore Street	76
Carter, High Street	35
Carter's, Temple Street	11
Church Street, by the Church	127 - 129
Co-op, Mill Street	144
Colwills, All Saints Road	132
Counter Tops, Temple Street	10
Cover Picture, Friths Post Card	
County Steam Laundry, Old Fore Street	109
Culverwell's, Fore Street	72
Davey's, High Street	27
Eveleigh, High Street	41
Fern, 38 Mill Street	146
Feoffees House, Mill Street	142
Fish, Temple Street	19
Grand Cinema, High Street	58
Green's. Fore Street	69
Hargreave's, Temple Street	20
Hartnell, D., Mill Street	144
Hayes Studio, High Street	45
High Street, Top of Holmdale	39
Hill, New Street	99
Home and Colonial, Fore Street	87
Horse and Groom, Russell Street	147
International, High Street	50
Irish, Spinning Wheel, Stead & Simpson	75
Irish Linen, High Street	64
Kandy Shop, Fore Street	66
Lennards, High Street	46
Leaving the Fire Station	62
London House, Spohr House	80
London Hotel, Fore Street	95
Lower Fore Street	82
Lower High Street	47
Lower Temple Street	13
Market Place	120
Martin - Late Smith, High Street	30
Milk Floats	7
Mill Street	139
Mill Street Corner with Holmdale	137 - 143
Mill Street, Nos. 17/18	142
Mitchell's, High Street	55
Myrtle Terrace	33
Northcott, Mill Street	140
O'Brien's, Prospect Place	118
Old Fore Street	106
Old Fore Street	103
Piper, Fore Street	70
Potburys and Cottage, High Street	51
Posta, High Street	34
Pepperell, Temple Street	18
Pepperell, New Street	96
Prospect Place	117
Radway Place	25
Rammell, High Street	44
Roxburgh Cottage, Russell Street	148
Santer & Sons, High Street	43
Sellek's, High Street	54
St. John, Selley's Yard	81
St. John Ambulance	77
Stead & Simpson to Knights, Fore Street	78
Tedbury's Milk Bar, Fore Street	68
Trump's Cafè, Fore Street	93
Trumps', Old Fore Street	104
Tucker, Temple Street	10
Upper High Street	60
Veal's Corner	86
Victoria Cottages, Temple Street	12
Whitton, Fore Street	67
Worlds Stores, High Street	52
Wymans, High Street	48

ADVERTISEMENTS

Bailey's, Temple Street	16
Barnard, Old Fore Street	112
Biarritz, Prospect Place	117
Biffen, High Street	49
Bond. M. G. Fore Street	70
Bookland, Market Place	113
Buxton, New Street	100
Bray, Old Fore Street	107
Bristol Boot Co., New Street	98
Burgoynes, High Street	56
Caseley, Russell Street	149
Collier and Son, Church Street	126
Coulson Stores	85
Culverwell's, Fore Street	72
Cummings', Hairdresser's. Fore Street	77
Don, Old Fore Street	111
Doyle, J., High Street	37
Drew, A. C., Old Fore Street	105
Ellis, A., High Street	38
Evis, Landpart	17
Gliddon and Son, Church Street	122
Hawkins, Walter, Fore Street	71
Huggett, Holmdale	138
Kirkpatrick-Smith, New Street	100
Lashbrook & Sons, Church Street	126
Leask & Co, Old Fore Street	106
Lee, H., Temple Street	8
London House, Fore Street	80
Martin, Mill Street	140
Mocha, Prospect Place	116
Opie's, New Street	100
Orman, Church Street	124
Orman's, Temple Street	20
Penberthy, Fore Street	74
Pepperell's Dairy, New Street	96
Perth Dye Works, Temple Street	21
Potbury & Sons, Winslade Road	15
Potbury & Sons, High Street	53
Prince & Vincent, High Street	63
Rickwoods', Prospect Place	119
Rodd, T. H., Fore Street	83
Sanders, Old Fore Street	102
Sellek, H., Fore Street	87
Spinks, Church Street	126
Spohr House, Fore Street	80
Tancock, Coach Builder, Church Street	128
Thomson, High Street	41
Town Brewery, High Street	50
Valet Cleaners, Old Fore Street	107
Vallance Brewery	22
Newman, Fore Street	65
White, East Street	138

INTRODUCTION

A new shop opened in Sidmouth? Now what was there before? Walking down the High Street to the sea front one can see new names, new or changed shop fronts. Some names have been here for years, Fords, High Street Dairy, Trumps, Potburys, Gliddons, Fields, Haymans and Deans. Many family names have been carried on by sons or daughters, whilst others have been only here for a few months. With my daughter Margaret we started listing all we could remember. The list grew longer and the number of files got bigger!

We started to see local people, always asking them if they could remember details of shops in the past. Many said: You will have to write a book, so we have!. We have mainly concentrated on compiling a list of the shops past and present, including snippets of history.

Sidmouth was once spelt as Sidemew,[1] and it was originally a small fishing village, described as one of the "chiefest fisher towns of the shire".[2] In 1630 it was described as being formerly a good seaport with boat building yards[3], the yards are now York Terrace. There was a harbour until it became choked with sand and pebbles[4]. In 1700 there were only one or two small cottages near the sea, the fishermen and workers cottages were set back in Western Town and Eastern Town. A Samuel Curwen, in 1776 mentioned Sidmouth as having about one hundred houses.[5]

The houses were nearly all built of grey stone or cob and thatched. In the later 16th century new thatched buildings were erected in Old Fore Street. In 1776 a few roofs consisted of Cornish slate and some of shingles [8]. The church had a slate roof.

In 1630 Sir William Polwhele described Sidmouth as being famous for its fishing and stating: "Fairs as holden in the market place on Easter Monday and Tuesday – the third Monday in September for cattle". [11]

In 1790 the main industries were fishing and dairy farming. Some butchers housed their cattle behind their shop premises, the cattle grazed in the pastures which are now Vicarage Road, The Lawn, Salcombe Road, Cotlands and The Byes.

In 1796, The Copper Plate Magazine stated, "The town is of late tolerably frequented in the bathing season, popularity as a holiday place has begun to develope".

The oldest parts of the town are Old Fore Street. (Forum Street), Church Street, Western town and Eastern town, all meeting at the Market Cross (Market Place). Later Fore Street and New Street were developed.

In medieval times Sidmouth had a Market. The first mention of the Market Cross is around 1175. There were sheds, shops and stalls at the market in 1220 [9]. In a deed of 1322 it was at the west end of the Market House. [10]

In a 1803 census there were about 240 houses and 1252 inhabitants [6]. Sidmouth was described as being "a small market town in a narrow valley. The little river Sid flows towards the ocean, lost in the pebbles on the beach. Now pleasure boats and fishing smacks can only land on the beach. Good accommodation, elegant ballroom, billiard room, and tea rooms. New lodging houses are being built near the sea". [7]

In 1810, the Rev. Butcher wrote that: "The main market days are Tuesday and Saturday, several Butchers and Bakers were in the town, a plentiful supply of Beef, Mutton and Pork, Bread and Cakes are supplied in abundance. Every day country people bring in supplies of poultry, eggs, etc., to the doors of the inhabitants. Vegetables and fruit are grown by gardeners around the town, early names; Arnoll, Barnet and Franklin. Fruit is also brought in from the neighboring parishes and even as far away as Taunton and other distant places."

The Sidmouth Journal reported on the 14th October, 1914. The early closing movement is having drawbacks in regard to Saturday nights, some of the shops are unable to close punctually at 9.00 p.m. owing to the people from the surrounding villages being unable to complete their shopping so early.

The early town started at the north end of the valley at Mill Cross (All Saints corner), and stretched for about one third of a mile to the sea, with lodging houses, shops and cottages, to the Market Place. The lower end of the town divided into two roads. Cheapside

(Fore Street) had the best shops and two Inns, the London and New Inn, and several lodging houses. Old Fore Street had a Post Office or Receiving Office, one Inn, and cottages. The west side of the town was called Western Town, where most of the old buildings of Sidmouth were to be found. The east side of the town was known as the Marsh and then Eastern Town.

The town grew up around the cottages. As trade increased the cottages became shops. Above the first floor level the external appearance of the buildings has hardly altered. On the ground floor the front room became the shop and the front door became the shop door, or a new doorway was put in. As trade improved further, the whole of the ground floor was amalgamated into the shop, with store and work rooms at the back or on the first floor. A number of cottages and houses were demolished in order to make way for new shops, pavements and road improvements. Now there is only one thatched roofed shop, the rest are now slated.

In 1837 private firms were supplying gas lighting for the town. In 1912 the council took over the gas firms. Electric street lighting started in November 1923.

There was a Toll gate at Turnpike Lane (bottom of Winslade Road), another at the bottom of Salcombe Road across the road by the bridge. This gate has now been built with stone pillars as the entrance to the Byes. The old entrance was a narrow path on the other side of the Toll House beside the river.

Some of the shops have changed many times, both in terms of their owners and their trades. Not all the shops are run by the owners. Shops often traded under their old names, even when the shop owners or managers have changed. A lot of trade in the town in the early days was carried out by workers in their own homes. Trades included lace making, boot and shoe work, leather goods, dress making and laundry, etc. Many shops used to have a sun blind over the pavement supported by upright poles fitted into holes in the kerb stones, some of these holes can still be seen along the pavements today.

The trade name that was over the shop, and/or the type of business, have been typed in CAPITALS. Other shop names, which we have not been able to accurately confirm are typed in lower case. The exact date the shop opened or changed hands has been very hard to trace, therefore some dates are only a guide as to when they were there. The shop numbers are as now, and the old numbers are in brackets. Each street is in order of a walk down one side and back the other side. There were also other small shops in the side roads or streets and these are listed at the end of the main streets.

Originally the Sid valley was composed of Woolbrook, Landpart and a Fishing town. Woolbrook was almost a separate community before you came to what we now call 'The top of the town', this part, known as Landpart, was not thought of as part of 'The Town', that started at Mill Cross and the Upper High Street. This was almost a separate community. Children from Western town, Eastern town and the Marsh did not often mix with children from Landpart, probably not many of the real old Sidmouthians came up this far from the sea front either. Vernon Bartlett wrote: "usually we Townies met our Landpart folk when they came to swim from the beach or to qualify for a hand out of herring or mackerel by helping to haul up the drifters or seine boats onto the beach, or at All Saints School." The ending of the Radway Estate and the infill of private houses and a few shops changed all this.

Now we will start our walk at the bottom of Winslade Road working our way down to the main streets along Temple Street, Vicarage Road, Radway into the main town.

TEMPLE STREET, EAST SIDE

The street still has mainly terraced houses on both sides of the road. The road down to about Water Lane was called "Landpart" and on down to Lawn Vista was Temple Street. Around 1910 it all changed to Temple Street.

Names of shopkeepers which we have not been able to place: Mr. Philip Evans, 1883 - 1889 listed as Bricklayer and Plasterer. Mr. Henry Miller, 1879 - 1890. Mr. James, Grocer, Tea Dealer, 1889 - 1914. William Price, 1893 - 1902.

Starting down the left side of the road towards the town, on past the turning to Sid Park Road.

118.   In 1906, Mr. F. Charles, Stone and Marble Mason, was in Radway Row. By 1919 he had moved to Landpart. In 1926 his address was Rockinham Villas and by 1934 was called the Western Memorial Co. Ltd. By 1947, Mr. and Mrs. Parnell. A new trade in 1979, HAIR FLAIR, Hairdressers.

116.   Eaton Farm Dairy. In 1889 a Mr. Frederick Farrant, cowkeeper and dairyman. Mr. Medhurst, before Mr. and Mrs. C. T. Baker who bought the business in October 1917, this became Eaton Farm Dairy and Grocers, W. H. BAKER by 1925. They had a herd of Devon and two Guernsey cows which were milked in buildings at the back of the shop. Next Mr. and Mrs. Whitehead opened as CLIFFORD'S, Grocery Stores in September 1959. In 1978 change of trade to become GEARBOX, Mike and Joan Welch.

114.   These buildings are behind the shops, through the arch-way, which was built high enough for the hay wagons to go through to the outbuildings at the rear of the shops. These started out as cow sheds and milking sheds for the cows, which were walked down Manstone Lane from fields up in Burscombe Lane. Later in the mid 1930s some of the buildings were taken down or altered to make seventeen new garages. It was then sold to a group of local dairymen, Baker, Elliott, Fisher, Hamblen, Hill, Orford and Tucker, to become Sidmouth Dairies, this was to enable them to deliver their milk around Sidmouth. The milk was collected in churns from the neighbouring farms and taken to Sidbury for treating and bottling and brought here for the roundsmen to deliver. They first had handcarts, called 'pedestrian controlled vehicles', they later had electric milk floats, and these were stored here and had to be charged up over-night. When the Sidbury depot was closed the equipment was brought here and all the treatment and bottling was down in the large building nearest the Byes. Several different names have run the business over the years Lastly under the name 'UNIGATE'.
In March 2001, the site was cleared for three town houses to be built.

Mrs. J. Ridley

R.. Spurway

Ron Spurway with the old and new milk floats

1.   Florence Villas. In 1893 - 1930s we have a reference for a Mr. James Pring, Boot and Shoe maker, possibly here, or in 78 or 72, as a house, not a shop. In 1935 to 1950, Mr. A. Sparkes, Boot and Shoe repairer, also as a Guest House.

78.   Mr. and Mrs. Hercules LEE, Ladies and Gents. Hosier and Outfitters in 1932. W. C. Freeman, Fish and Chip Saloon in 1947. C. T. Petherick in the 1950s. Temple Cafe in 1968 to 1999, when it closed. The ground floor and shop front changed to become a private house.

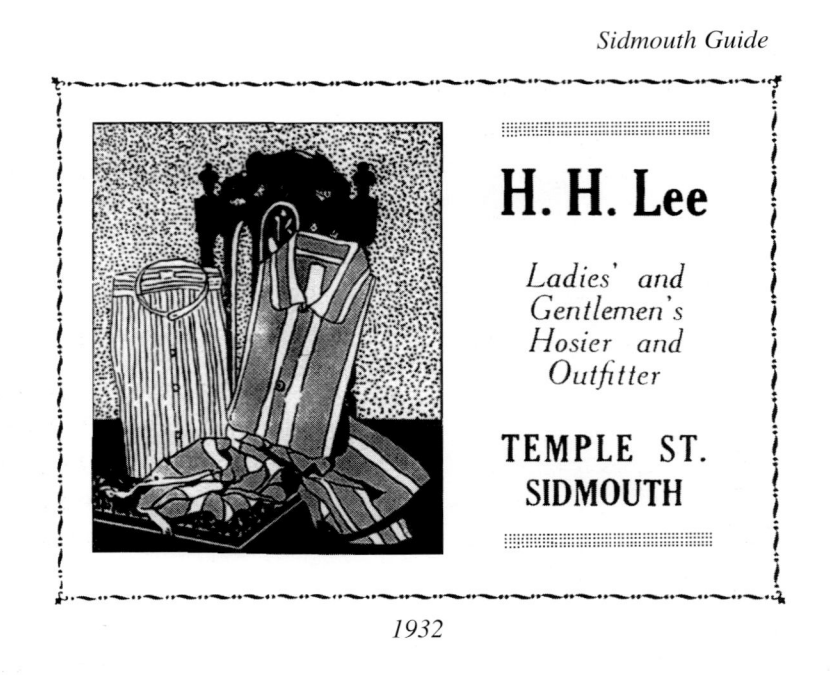

Sidmouth Guide

H. H. Lee

Ladies' and Gentlemen's Hosier and Outfitter

TEMPLE ST. SIDMOUTH

1932

74.   (1) Co-operative Society, Grocery Department, 1920s to 1968. The manager for many years was Mr. Ron Jordan. Sidmouth Pottery in the early 1980s. Now OXFAM, Charity Shop.

72.   (2) The Co-operative Society, Drapery Department in 1930. By 1951 the shop name changed to E. and G. Filkins, Drapers, also Taxis. By 1968, Mr. A Scott, Proprietor, Cowdrey Hardware. Next Wades, Wine making equipment, Pets and Gardens. 1982. HOME & GARDENS. Then Mr. Davies, Pet Foods, Homes and Garden shop. Now called SIDMOUTH PET AND GARDEN.

70.   (3) Mr. Lewis Tucker, Fruiterer in 1923. Next, EFFIE TUCKER. Fruiterer and Florist. 1939 - 1952. Taken on by Norman Carter, Greengrocers. to 1998, keeping the name Effie Tuckers. In 1999, new shopkeeper, Mr. Waring, Greengrocer.

68. The corner shop always seems to have been a butchers. The first name which we have is that of Mr. Swain who was here in 1910 - 1926. At the rear of the shop was their slaughter house. Another name connected to these premises is a Mr. Percy Annis, here in 1934. He sold the shop to a Mrs. Squire and Mr. J. Norman, in the 1940s Then in the early 1950s, the LISTER Family, later Mr. and Mrs. Richards. On August 1st 1976, three brothers, Chris, Martin and Phillip Long, bought the business and opened as LONG BROS. BUTCHERS.

We walk on past two cottages and the turning into Water Lane. We come to the first of a row of shops to what is now the Volunteer Inn car park.

62. This corner with Water Lane was a builder's yard belonging to Mr. Frank Baker. He built the shop in 1933. Opening as HARGREAVE'S STORES, Grocers. Mr. and Mrs. Baker, unrelated to the builder. Mr. Baker Sub Post Office in 1935 as well as grocers. Next it became CAROUSEL, nearly new - bric-a-brac, Mrs Maunder, opened in July 1985 to 1997. The premises are no longer used as a shop.

The next two shops were built in the late 1930s, first number 60 and later 58.

60. The first name we have found for here is Sergeant Reed, Butchers, in 1939. Followed by DOBSONS, Tie Maker, in 1947. The shop was unoccupied in 1949. The next name is Harry WOOLCOTT, Furnishers, Mr. and Mrs. Chapman in 1950. Mrs Laverick, Men's Outfitters, 1968 - 1970s. Mr. Peter Richard's, Shoes in 1979. In 1981 new owners and trade, Mr. Bill Lankester, J.K.L., Electrical, T V and Video Library. Now J. K. L. SALES AND SERVICE, Electrical goods.

58. The first names for here are, Charles F. Devereux, Drug Store and Hairdressers in 1937 and Elaine's Ladies Hairdresser both here until about 1947. Norman Cook, Hairstylist in the late 1970s, and later it was Jane Rattue, Hairdressers. In 1989 the premises were taken over by J. K. L. with their shop next door.

56. TUCKER BROTHERS in 1920s. Next it became The MODEL DAIRY. They had two large counters facing the door. The two large slate counter tops are now a garden ornament in a local back garden. Next as Hammetts Dairies. Then to SIDMOUTH DAIRIES by 1947 to 1970. The next trade was Furniture and Carpets, G. M. WRAY, closing in 1998. The front of the building has hardly changed over the years, the shop front and the glazed tiles are still here today. In December 2000 Becky Robson opened as THE HAIR TEMPLE, Hairdressers.

J. Ankins

Slate Counter Tops, M. Tucker

M. Tucker

56 Temple Street

Edward, Connie, Stan Tucker and an apprentice

54.   HINTON LAKE and Son, Chemist, 1926 - 1968. Various managers: Mr. Fish, Mr. Tooze, Mr. Sharlor. Changed to CARTER'S, Furnishings, Carpets, moving to here in 1970 when their High Street shop closed. On June 17th, 2000 they closed down. In May 2001 the shop was refurbished and opened as THE PAINTED HOUSE.

J. Ankins

May 1999. Shops numbers 62 to 54

On site of the Volunteer Car Park there used to be six small cottages called 'Victoria Cottages'. Two faced onto the road with a wide covered way through the end cottage to the other cottages, and the Vet's work place and stables at the back. Number 6 used to be the Vet's house, Veterinary Surgeon's. The first Vet's name we have found is George Sumption 1866. Followed by William Summers in 1883 - 1890. W. H. James, 1923. Mr. P. G. Steele, 1940. Steele and Wardrop, 1950. Number 3 was Miss Clode, a Servants Registry Office in 1930 - 1939. On the end of the row of cottages was a Garage and Petrol Pump run by Mr. Wright in the 1920s later used by the pub as a store. The Vet's Surgery moved to Chandler's Lane when the cottages were demolished.

J. Ankins

January 1960, Victoria Cottages

52.   THE VOLUNTEER INN.

46.   (2) Mr W. Farrant & Sons, Paint, Wallpaper, Painters and Shop in 1893 - 1940. C. W. Halse, Cycle Shop, around 1947 - 1949. In 1950 J. Roberts, Radio and Electrical Dealer. Another change of trade to a D.I.Y. Shop Mr. Clutton, in the 1960s. They were also an agency for parcels for Devon General Bus Company, closing at the end of 1998. Now a private house.

40.   Police Station. Built about 1910.

28.   PINNEY & SONS, Builders, Office and Workshop, to January 1991. It then changed to BEWES, Builders, Elysian Works.

24.   (11) John Cload, Pork Butcher 1890 - 1919. Mrs. Cload, General Shopkeeper. Mrs. Amelia Jeffery, July 1925, The Doll Shop. In 1935 Mr. F. D. Jeffery ran a daily motor carrier service to Exeter. By 1939 he had moved to Ravenscrag in Vicarage Road. Also here the Singer Sewing Machine Co. Ltd., in 1935 - 1939. Sidmouth Dental Laboratory, Mr. and Mrs. Channing, 1947, and then a change of trade to Fruit and Vegetables in 1949. Now back to a private house.

18.   (8) Mrs Amelia Jeffery's General Stores 1930. Mr A. G. Rogers, Grocer 1936 - 1951. Continental, Greengrocer. Winifred's, General Store, 1968. This shop was often empty for several months; trades never seemed to stay here for long, by 1982 it had become a Chiropodist Surgery, TEMPLE STREET CLINIC. G. M. Smith, Chiropody. By 1999 with S. King and P. Sturgess, Acupuncturist Osteopath.

Lower Temple Street

16.   (7)   Miss Mary L Churchill's, Drapery Store, 1919 - 1935. Mr. and Mrs. Bellworthy in 1936. Private House.

14.   (6)   In 1930, Miss Churchill's. M. L. Comer, Fancy Draper. 1936-1951. THE REMNANT SHOP, E. A. White, Textiles 1951-1968: Victoria Bookshop, 1975. Shop now closed.

12   (5)   Albert Snell, Tobacconist, 1923. Mrs. E. D. Dowell, Sweet Shop, Confectioner, also C. J. Dowell, Motor Carriers, in 1926. The shop taken over by Mrs. G. Harden about 1932 - 1939. Mrs. Betty Pinney, Tobacconist and Confectioner. 1951. MacDonald, MAC'S Sweet shop and Tobacconist in 1955 to the late 1960s. Sidmouth Old Books, Adrian and Molly Lee, to 1988. Second hand book shop to 1995. Now empty.

8.	(4) Miss Mary Lake, Corset Maker, 1923 - 1931. Courtney Dowell Jn., Carrier, 1935 - 1939. Printing Business started by George Taylor. He was in Eastern Town in 1939 before moving to here with R. H. Grattan on the Handicraft side, The SIDMOUTH PRINTING WORKS and HANDICRAFTS Ltd. For many years a Foyles Lending Library was run from these premises, and then Mr. Taylor became unable to continue with the lending library and it was taken on by Schofields in their shop. Later just called SIDMOUTH PRINTING WORKS Ltd. When the handicraft side of the business was dropped. Mr. Taylor sold the business to Mr. T. Lightfoot. They moved to the former Devon Conversion unit on the Alexandria Industrial Estate in May 1981. Then this became The SOVEREIGN GROUP, Printers. Now a private house.

6.	(3) Freddie Goss, Blacksmith in 1897, also Plumbers by the 1900s. In 1910 Mr. Frederick T. DUNN, (Stan), Plumbers, Ironmongers, Builders. In 1919 Stan Dunn's sister Dolly looked after the shop, into the 1950s. The shop then changed to Lewis Russell, Ironmonger. By 1966 it became BOND and FINNIMORE, Builders, Plumbers and Ironmongers. Then changed to a Computer Shop to January 1985. Hugh Symons, Microfilm Services, paperwork and documents onto microfilm, October 1989.

TEMPLE STREET, WEST SIDE

Mates Guide

POTBURY & SONS, Auctioneers, House & Estate Agents, and Valuers.

REMOVAL CONTRACTORS and Insurance Agents.

Full particulars of all Furnished or Unfirnished Houses, or Properties for Sale sent on application.

Furniture and Luggage Warehoused in their Repository specially built for that purpose

Offices and Showrooms: **HIGH STREET, SIDMOUTH.**

1907

Starting again from Winslade Road on the right hand side we come to the entrance to Potbury's yard and auction rooms. This was milking sheds and yards, the cows walked in from fields (now Yard Hill), the milk was sold in Fern Cottage by a Mr. Fern.
Potbury's first furniture wagons were drawn by horses, and these were stabled here, and known as 'The Pound'. In the late 1920s they built a Repository, entrance from Winslade Road. Potburys built new Auctions Rooms and altered the entrance from Temple Street in April 1985, after being in Mill Street (the Old School) for 38 years.

143.   Continuing down the road, we reach the first shop. The Modern Fish and Chip Cafe, TANZILLI'S, Mr. Tanzilli and his son came from Italy in the 1930s. Mr. Pearse ran the shop in the war years about the 1940s. Next it became Chicos in the early 1980s. In the 1990s it was called The First and Last Fish Bar. Now called TOP WOK, Chinese Take-away.

After the entrance to the Cemetery, where the Spar car park is now, this was a market garden. Mr. Clark in the 1920s, also called Landpart Nurseries.

129.   Fuchsia Cottages. There were three cottages here, next to H. G. Dean's Bakery, (127). In 1962 Mr. Harry Dean died and Gerald Dean demolished the cottages and built onto Dean's Bakery and Shop. This was the first self-service store in Sidmouth, called SUPERSTORES, a VIVO store. In 1968 the store was extended to its present size and by 1973 called SPAR.

127.   This building may have been John Miller, Baker in 1850s before the present business which was founded by Mr. Ruben Dean, a Baker who moved here from Branscombe in 1872. One of his sons, William, had taken over by 1910, and later his brother Harry George after the 1914/18 War. By 1928 Mr. H. F. Dean had opened another shop in the High Street (see next to Woolworths) selling goods baked here in the bakery, which was at the back of the shop. There were two steam tube ovens and a very old stone built flue oven which was heated by burning wood faggots inside, then raked out, the heat in the stone being sufficient to bake with. Mr. Dean first used a pony and trap for deliveries and his son Gerald a tricycle. In 1955 Mr. Gerald Dean with his father Harry decided to start selling grocery items and then the new idea of a self-service select, but only a new bakehouse was built. Miss Quaintance worked in the shop for many years. The bakery ceased production in 1962.

In 1973 the first change of trade here to a TOY SHOP run by Mrs. Dean until 1977. The shop then closed and became Offices for the Supermarket. It became a shop again with Mr. and Mrs. Gedgeway opening a D.I.Y. Shop. Next a wool shop and then in November 1989 called SHEEP'S CLOTHING. Closed in 1993 and now reverting back to a private cottage.

109.   (1) Eaton Terrace. In 1928 a shop was made by taking in part of the front garden. This has always been a newsagents' shop, John C. BAILEY, Newsagents, Tobacconist, Confectioners with a Circulating Library in 1931. Les Eaton then took over the shop to 1946 also selling toys to 1966. The name changed to MEESON for a time then MARTIN Newsagents. In March 2000 Peter and Janet Sullivan took over and renamed it TEMPLE STREET NEWS.

107.   Eaton House. In 1852, this may have been, John Holmes, Shopkeeper, Draper and Grocer. In 1878 it was in a directory as

BAILEY'S TEMPLE STREET LANDPART

Newsagents, Booksellers, Stationers, Tobacconists, ∴ Confectioners,

∴   CIRCULATING LIBRARY   ∴

Agent for all Sunday Papers

We give prompt and early delivery of all Daily and Sunday Papers to all parts of Town and District.   Personal attention to all orders.

A Trial Solicited.   Telephone 317

1932

John Holmes, Shopkeeper and Carpenter. It was not until 1930 that we find an entry for Frederick Holmes, Butchers in Temple Street. Mr. J. White was the manager in 1937. Mr. Frank Newton in the 1960s, Mr. Pope followed by Mr. Lewis. The shop floor used to be covered in sawdust, the wooden chopping bench 'counter' was on the left-hand side, and the 'pay desk' in the back corner, and a refrigeration unit at the back of the shop. The shop kept the name HOLMES until it changed to Howard's Woodcraft in the late 1960s-1970. The initials 'F H' still there in mosaic tiles in the shop doorway. Next became GEDGEWAY, D I Y Shop, by 1982. This in turn changed to LAYZELLS, Building materials, General D I Y shop, in February 1988.

93.   In from the main street behind the shops was an area called Sandpits or Maeer's Yard. Mr. John Maeer started a coal delivery business in East Street and his son George carried this on with a Haulage Contractor's business, with two or three lorries. First it was horse drawn carts. The horses were called; Colonel, Mabel and Madam, and kept in a field over the river near Sid Lane. The sand was dug and sieved by hand and loaded onto tipping carts. Mr. George Maeer retired in 1981. Miller and Lilley took over and stopped using this site. They carried on from the Station Yard. Also in here are 1 and 2 Sandpit Cottages. In the 1920s No. 1, Mr. White and No. 2, Miss Cawley, who sold fish and chips at the back of the cottage. The cottages are still here. In July 1985 the site was built on to make thirty-one flats called Temple Gardens.

89 and 91. (5 and 6). Princes Row.
(6)   This was the end cottage after the entrance to Sandpits. We have a reference for Joseph Mortimore, Tailor, in Temple Street in 1906-1910 he may have been here as another reference is for 'Chip' Mortimore, wet Fish Shop here, but no date. This cottage had a small extension built out onto the front garden to make a shop. From about 1929 it was Mr. Charles Evis, Gentlemen's Hairdresser. Mr. and Mrs. Evis lived in number 5. Most of the school boys had their hair cut here, usually on a Friday. It was often a race from Woolbrook School to get in first after school. Mr. Evis would shout at the boys if they made too much noise whilst they waited their turn. In about 1964 Mr. C. Male and in 1974 Mr. Clyde Cann, Hairdresser, who stayed here until the shop closed. The entrance to the Sand Pit was very narrow, the shop window often showed signs of being hit by lorries turning in and out from the main road. The shop and cottage were demolished to make a wider entrance and road for the flats in June 1985.

EVIS
LANDPART

Hairdresser etc.

Give Evis a trial for a Quick and Easy Shave.

Advertisement 1931

Further on down the road past Ascerton Road, we come to a tall detached building with three shops on the ground floor, Gorse View, Ashley House and Alexandra House.

V. Fish

71.　　Gorse View. There was a George Pepperell, Farmer in 1875 and a Mr. Pepperell living in Jubilee Terrace in 1880. He then opened a shop here, PEPPERELL DAIRY, until he moved to the Market Place. By 1902 it had changed to a Grocer's Shop, James Thomas Bird, Baker and Post Office. Next became Mr. Isaac Hargreaves, in 1919, Grocer and Post Office, Mrs. Ruth Hargreaves, 1923 - 1932. Mr. Rabey, Post Master, he moved to Market Street in 1938. Next the Army & Navy Stores, Mr. and Mrs. H. C. Trickey, 1939 - 1950s. New trade, Mr. V. FISH, Cycle Shop, moved here from his workshop in Elim Villas, Peasland Road.

V. Fish

1968

69.   Ashley House. In 1905 Landpart Stores, Howard Brothers, Grocers and Post Office. Mr. Frank Baker bought the shop and kept the name HARGREAVE'S STORES Ltd. Family Grocers, they then had both shops, until they moved to their new shop on the other side of the road in 1933. The shop then became Tucker & Son, Ironmongers. They were in Holmdale in 1930, and opened here by 1935. In 1949 they moved to Fore Street. Next trade here was Mr. Len Burch, Radio Shop. Mr. Burch had 69 and 67 for a time. Then Mr. Trickey, Clothes shop in the 1950s. Next change to JOSMAN WINDOWS and DOORS.

67.   Drapery House. James Gill LOVERIDGE, Cash Draper in 1902. Agent for R. P. Campbell 'The Perth Dye Works'. By 1910 he had moved to Fore Street. Then it became, Alexandra House. Wallace Beech, Hairdresser in 1925 to 1934 when he moved to the Grand Cinema. Then Miss Orman, Ladies Hairdresser, to be followed by Mr. Hicks, Hairdresser, 1937. In March 1938 he moved to Vicarage Road.

M. Baker

1933

Sidmouth Observer

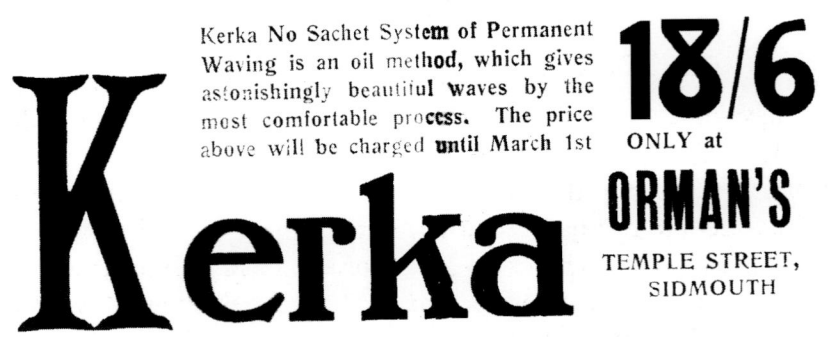

Kerka No Sachet System of Permanent Waving is an oil method, which gives astonishingly beautiful waves by the most comfortable process. The price above will be charged until March 1st

Kerka

18/6 ONLY at

ORMAN'S
TEMPLE STREET,
SIDMOUTH

Eugene Waving at Church Street,

1934

Then changed to F. J. Tucker & Sons, Plumbers, in 1939. Mr. Len BURCH, Radio Shop in 1950 to 1980. On the end wall of the building at first floor level, looking down the road was a large advert painted on the wall 'L.BURCH, Radio Shop'. Next it became an Antiques shop for a short time. Then a Tool Hire business to 1984. Change of trade, The UPPER CRUST, Confectioners, opened in August 1985 to 1986. Now the shop window has been taken out and inside converted to a private House.

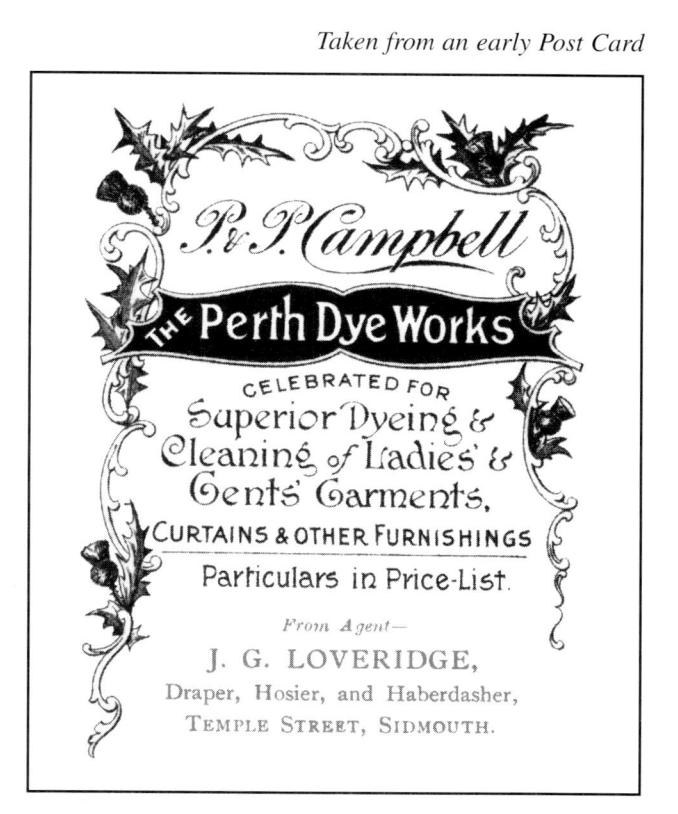

Taken from an early Post Card

P. & P. Campbell
THE Perth Dye Works
CELEBRATED FOR
Superior Dyeing &
Cleaning of Ladies' &
Gents' Garments,
CURTAINS & OTHER FURNISHINGS
Particulars in Price-List.
From Agent—
J. G. LOVERIDGE,
Draper, Hosier, and Haberdasher,
TEMPLE STREET, SIDMOUTH.

Further down the road, past the terrace houses was the site of the Brewery. Mr. Richard A. Searles in 1830 and Thomas Searles in 1836. In 1874 it was Harvey and Vallance, Brewers and by 1890, VALLANCE'S BREWERY. Brewing days were Tuesdays and Fridays, as all the nearby neighbours could tell, depending on the wind direction. They were a large firm employing up to forty people and had their own lorries at one stage. Later it stopped making beer, changing to a bottling plant. They also were Corn and Seed Merchants in the early days, and Coal Merchants with a delivery round. Changed to Devenish and Co. Ltd., and later to Greenalls. All demolished in 1980. In 1981 on Thursdays a one day market was held, which ran for about eight weeks, Now a block of flats, Homemeadows.

Down the road past Brewery Lane was a large red brick house, which was said to have been built for a Station Hotel in 1876. It comprised of twelve bedrooms, cellars, coach house and stables. As far as we can find out it was called The Bricklayers Arms,[12] It was advertised as for sale in February 1876, as a freehold property, with a frontage of one hundred and seventeen feet. In 1880 to about 1925 it was a boys' Grammar school run by Mr. Jago. Later it became Potbury's Furniture Repository. It was demolished and the site became terrace houses called Fairlawn Court.

Further down the road we cross over Elysian Fields Driveway to a new building. Apollonia House, Dentist Surgery, built in 1974.

The name of the road changes to VICARAGE ROAD.

One Shop between Victoria Road and Connaught Road. D. J. Hicks, Ladies' and Gentlemen's Hairdresser. 1939 - 1960s. C. J. Walker, Opticians, OPTOMETRISTS.

On the corner with Connaught Road, a new building, The British (Connaught) Restaurant, opened in October 1943. After the war it was used by the Catholic Church for meetings and Church functions. Site was later cleared and St. Teresa's Hall was built in 1961 and opened in 1964.

Crossing over Connaught Road. On the corner going down the road was TOMALIN'S GARAGE, Edward A. Tomalin, proprietor, 1937. Then became REED MOTORS, 1968. By 1987 A.T.S Garage and Tyre Specialist.

Next is a large brick building, built by Pinney & Sons and opened on February 24th, 1938 as the main Post Office and Sorting Office. The Post Office side was closed in 1991, moving into Fords Shop. Now The Loft Club, a teenage drop in centre.

Sidmouth Observer

WHEN VISITING SIDMOUTH

Try

"G. M."

Vallances Gold Medal Ale

Winner of Champion Gold Medal—London.

THE FINEST ALE IN
THE WEST COUNTRY

VALLANCES SIDMOUTH BREWERY

BREWERS, WINE & SPIRIT MERCHANTS

Phone : 72

Coal, Coke, Anthracite & Logs

Best possible value for all descriptions.
Delivered free from small.

G. VALLANCE

Phone : 72

COAL MERCHANT   SIDMOUTH

1932

After the turning into Radway Road, the first building is called Salcombe View and is comprised of six flats with shops on the ground floor called Radway Place.

The first shop on the corner site, was INDDEN & HARRIS, a Dress Shop in the 1920s. Then the BON MARCHÉ, Mrs. J. Darwin, Ladies Outfitters, December 1929. Next HAROLD TRICKEY, Army and Navy stores to 1939 when he moved to Temple Street. Followed by Ferris & Prescott, Ladies Outfitters in 1946, and A. S. Ferris by 1947. CAVENDISH HOUSE, Drapers 1954. HAROLDS, Mens Outfitters which closed in 1990. New Trade, Mr. Chris Taylor and Mr. Carlton Leworthy opened as C & C, Electrical in July 1990.

The next shop down was occupied by Mrs. M. Reed, Fruit and Flowers in the 1930s. By 1935 Alfred Kensdale, later Mr. W. E. Kensdale, Fruiterer, 1946. J. S. Scott in 1958 - 1968. Later called Radway Stores, around 1988. When the Radway Stores closed, there was a change of trade. For a short period of time, around 1995, the shop sold Garden ornaments. In 1995 Mr. R. ROGERS, Green Grocer, opened, having moved from the High Street, closing down in October, 1999. In 2000 opened as NATURAL STYLE, closing in May 2001. On 7th June, Gillian Ivey, opened as SID VALLEY PETS.

The next business we come to before the Cinema was the RADWAY CAFÉ. Miss L. Gilpin, Confectionery and Café in 1937. FORTE'S, Café and Restaurant, around 1948. JILLS RESTAURANT in the 1970s. GOURMET GRUB, Restaurant opened in May 1985. CADILLAC, Restaurant and Cafe, 1989. In November 1996 after an interior update reopened as DI PAOLA'S, La Cucina Italiana Restaurant, Philip and Gina Eldon, closing in January 2000. In August, Mr. Neil Harding opened a Seafood Restaurant, NEIL'S RESTAURANT.

The Radway Theatre opened in June 1928. In August 1936 The Palace Cinema, by 1937 called The Palace Picture House, Mr. A. W. Ellis. Now The Radway Cinema.

The building on the corner of All Saints Road was a large private semi-detached house. "Sidlands" and "Sidlands Lodge". The entrance to Sidlands was near where the Radway Cinema is now. It then changed to The Constitutional Club A.A.C. in about 1909 when they moved from the Town Hall, which was in the Old Market House. This in turn became the Conservative Club. Sidlands Lodge had an entrance on the corner with All Saints Road, where the seat is now, with large wooden gates hung on two large square pillars with a concrete ball on the top. This became a doctor's surgery, Dr. Michelmore. In the late 1950s The Conservative Club took it over with Sidlands. It is now all the Conservative Club.

Crossing over the road to the East side we come to the RADWAY INN.

The next few shops from the Inn to Newtown are also called Radway Place. Looking at the buildings now it looks as though they were built as five shops, but were originally numbered 1 to 11, as cottages or houses and were later all changed into the shops. Recorded in the Sidmouth Journal in October 1886; No. 2 and 3 for sale. No 2, Mr. Avery. No 3,

Miss Godfrey. Both had a back and a very small front gardens. Bought by Mr. B. Butter, a builder. The front doors were up two steps from the pavement, with a bow-fronted window set out from the front line of the building with a narrow flat roof.

The first names which we have found are,

(1)   Mr. Thomas Butter, he had a ninety acre farm employing two labourers, in 1851. George Elliot, Carpenter and H. Edwards, Stay Maker, both here in 1857. Miss Butter in 1866. Miss Miller, Lace and Laundry, 1897 - 1906.

(2)   Mr. Charles Farrant, Gardener in 1851. Edward Barratt, General Tailor here 1857 - 1892. In 1883 it must have changed into a shop, Mr. G. Avery, Grocer. He was also the receiver for the old Devon and Exeter Savings Bank, which opened on Tuesday and Friday evenings. Mr. A. Gooding, Pork Butcher, 1897 -1906.

(3)   Elizabeth Evans, Lace in 1857. W. H. Drew, Coal Merchant, 1868 -1870. A Lodging House in 1901 and we also have the name Smyth, Lodging House. In 1910 (as a shop), Mr. Ernest R. Bunker, Cycle Agent. Then Mr. Bunker, selling Sweets and Confectionery, until 1919 when it was taken over by Mrs. Emily Field and later by her son Harold by 1923, the shop was called FIELDS. Harold altered the inside of the shop, lowering the floor and fitting a new shop window. [13].The name changed with new owners to RADWAY STORES in the 1950s. In 1981 it was called RADWAY FINE ARTS and JEWELLERY. About 1984 F. McMURRAY traded here, changing to ACQUISITIONS, Fine Arts and Jewellery in 1985. The premises became a Coffee House in July 1987, trading as MAGPIE. In 1991 it became RADWAY CRAFTS. Then RADWAY CRAFTS AND TEA ROOM in 1992 and to THE TWO MAGPIES June 1995. The business closed in May 1996. In May 1997 it became ALI'S, Charcoal Grill. The name changed to, The TURKISH KEBAB, August 1999.

(4)   Mr. Robert Daniells, Master Builder 1851. Mr. or Mrs. Godfrey, Lodging House, 1857. In 1870 Miss L. Evans, Lace Maker,

(5)   Mrs. Jane Spencer, Lace Maker 1851. E. Miller, Shopkeeper and Lace Maker 1857 and then Mr. R. Miller, who was still here in 1890, 'Aerated Bread Depot'. The house was for sale in April 1903 and was bought by Mr. Williams. Mr. Rasmussen (a Belgian refugee), Greengrocer about 1910. Violet Houghton, Greengrocer in 1914. Changed to a Boot shop, W. R. MARTIN (nickname 'Pincher') here in 1926 to 1946. W. H. SADLER, Jeweller 1947 - 1952. SAVRY'S, Delicatessens, the earliest date which we have is 1958. On to Mr. POTTER in the late 1960s. TREASURE CHEST, Antiques in 1966 to October 1970. Then change to HARTNELL, Fresh Food. The shop closed in April 2000, keeping a delivery service.

(6)   Mrs. Mary Gooding, Lace Maker in 1851. Miss A.Paddon about 1870.

(7)   Miss Elizabeth Gale, Annuitant 1851. Mr. Robert Daniels, Builder, 1857. We have the name Albert Fulford, in Mill Street, as a Hairdresser in 1906 and for Umbrellas in 1910. The first date which we have for here as a shop is 1914, FULFORDS and Co. trading in Umbrellas and Fruiterers, Florists and Tobacconist to 1939. Next Mr. and Mrs. L. MILLER, Tobacco, Confectioners, in 1940s - 1950s. In 1970, PIERCE, Pottery, Tobacconist and Antiques. Around 1979, THE ZEBRA, Confectionery, Tobacco to July 1981. Next Mr. J. GOSLING, Gifts, Confectionery and Smoking accessories to 1984. In 1985, Jeanelle, this shop we have been unable to find the trade or any details. 1987 COUNTY KITCHENS and BATHROOMS. Then a change of trade to TANDOORI Indian Restaurant and Takeaway in June 1991. In November 2001, taken over by Showkatui Islam Chowdhury and his wife Salma.

(8)   Mr. Elijah Evans in 1851, a Mason employing two men and two boys. Mr. C. Farrant, Shoe Maker in 1857 -1868.

(9)   Mr. Thomas Wilmot in 1851. Mr. Simon Seaward, Builder. Later it became a shop. The first trader which we have been able to find is Mr. and Mrs. F. Fayer, LITTLE COVENT GARDEN, Fruiter, they were here in 1946. The early 1950s, WESSEX CLEANERS. The Shop was for sale in 1970. In the mid 1970s to early 1980s, called BULLDOG. Next ROY, Tropical Live Fish. HAIRWAYS about 1982. Then HEADLINERS in 1985.

(10)   Miss Susan Haydon, Annuitant in 1851. Mr. T. Butter, Farmer, Corn Dealer, Carpenter, Builder 1857 - 1878.

Post Card

Radway Place about 1914

(11)   Mr. Summers, Carpenter, in 1851. Number 10 became a shop by 1909, and number 11, by 1906.

The first shop, SCHOFIELD'S. Mr. Ralph Schofield, Hardware Dealer, in 1909 and later a Stationers and Newsagents, managed by Ralph and his wife. Ralph was killed in 1918 and his wife carried on the business. She also had a Circulating Library in 1931. The next change in the late 1960s was to PERCIVALS and in 1996 to NEWS PLUS.

The other shop was Mrs. Smith, Cycle Dealer in 1906. Mr. Albert Benjamin Smith was also listed as a cycle dealer in Holmdale in 1906. By 1919 it was Mr. CLAUD MARTIN, Bicycle shop. In 1923 traded as a Motor Engineer. When he closed it was taken over by Schofield's becoming one large shop.

Now we come to the turning to Newtown, and the start of High Street.

Sidmouth Herald

Radway Place, 1981

HIGH STREET, EAST SIDE

Crossing over the turning to Newtown, we come to the top end of the High Street. (Previously known as Upper High Street)

The first building on the corner with Newtown was a Private House, Miss Gertie Drew, Teacher at All Saints Girls School early 1900s. Later the ground floor was made into a shop (No. 142) with flats over the shop.

Miss Riley

Davey's October 1970

142.   No names or dates until Alan Mitchell, Hairdresser in 1937. He was in Mill Street in 1935. Next as VENITA, Ladies Hair Dressers in the 1960s. In 1970 the shop door was blocked up and this part taken into the next shop (140) as a new restaurant, NEW FRIENDS.

140.   In 1850 Elizabeth and John Holmes, Shopkeepers. No other names until Mr. George Edwin Illsley, as an apartment in 1897 and as a Boot Maker in 1902, to the late 1930s. It then must have been made into a shop. Mr. H. T. DAVEY and SONS, Fish and Poultry Merchants. This comprised two shop fronts with a central shop door. The left side, Fish, and the right side Green Grocery. In the early 1970s Mr. Kitin Lee made it a Chinese Restaurant called NEW FRIENDS. It is now called SILVER KING, and is still a restaurant.

Next down the road near this site in the 13th Century was an Old Mill. The land was owned by Adam de Radway. (Various spellings; Radeways, Radewies). By a deed in the Otterton Cartulary, John, Prior of Otterton and his Monks had a dispute with Adam de Radway. The case was tried at Exeter. The Prior had to pay Adam twenty shillings and stipulated to give him sixteen pence year besides; to quit-claim four pence a year levied on Adam's land. to grant him the right to grinding his corn first. The building is described as two mills under one roof [13]. Also two houses in a hollow with a descending flight of steps down to a basement. By about 1795 the mill was falling into decay, but still had the water wheel. The wheel was driven by the stream that ran down Mill Lane (All Saints Road). The mill was burnt down in 1847. According to Gerald Gibbens 'by a drunken coachman using a candle' [15]. Several old houses were also destroyed in this fire on the 8th December. A new mill was built in Mill Street by the river. The site is now Fords Shop.

Next there were two small shops with a small gap before the next building.

Mr. Walter Sellek, Butchers shop in 1851. Charles Purcell, Grocer about 1881, by1893 the name Mrs. Elizabeth Purcell to 1897. Mr. L. J. Mills, Cabinet Maker about 1902. In 1935 Mr. John David Sellek, Plumbers and Ironmongers to the 1940s, Radway Stores, Mr. and Mrs. G. Norman, Peter Norman, Sports in 1953.

The last two shops here, Sidmouth CHINACRAFT and GIFTWARE, next door to Mr. M. SHERWOOD, Chemist, both closed in May 1970.

This block was modernised, the front and interior rebuilt with three large windows on the first floor and as one large shop on the ground floor, with new entrance doors, for FORD and SON; Ironmongers and Televisions. This was one of the few town buildings to be changed completely. Most of the fronts of the buildings and roofs around the town have remained about the same from first floor level.

Next were three small shops.

Steven Hayman, Whitesmith in 1830, Ironmonger and Plumbers in 1836. By 1878, Mrs. Mary R. Hayman, Furnishing Ironmonger, Lamp and oil dealer and William, Plumber and Gasfitter. By 1906 Frank Hayman, Ironmongers.

Henry Curtis, Plumbers and Gas fitters in 1849. Mr. Arthur Curtis, bought the premises by auction on the 29th April 1879 for £160. The Curtis family were still trading here in 1916.

132.	By 1919 all three shops were made into one shop so it became No. 132, for Mr. Gilbert Ford, FORD and SON, Ironmongers and Plumbers. Mr. Owen Ford Ltd. Co. 1959. Later with Radio, TV, Electrical, Video library; Kitchens and Bathrooms.
The end part of the shop near the archway was made into IDEAS; Clothing Accessories in October 1986. ANTIQUE MARKET February 1988. SIDMOUTH WINDOW CENTRE in 1990. The WINE SELLER in 1994. The PHOTO SHOP, 1998. All under the name of FORDS. In 1991 part of the back of the shop became the GENERAL POST OFFICE.

Next down from Fords is an archway between the shops. At the back of the shops there used to be cow pens, stables and yard. Later made into workshops and stores. Water came from a well drawn up by a long handled cast iron pump shared by shops on both sides of the yard.

128.	Mr. Summers in 1851. James PEPPERELL, Dairy, 1857 to 1890. Mr. James Pepperell had the first horse drawn milk cart in Sidmouth. These carts were made by Venn Caseley, a coach builder who had a workshop and yard in Russell Street. They were designed to take the large galvanised brass rimmed milk churns. By 1839, Mr. Frederick Maeer's Dairy, then THE HIGH STREET DAIRY, Mr. and Mrs. W. A. Maeer in the early 1900s. Freddy Maeer's two daughters, Nell and Edie worked at the back of the shop and his brother went round the town with his pony. "Blossom" delivering the milk [16]. Mr. and Mrs. Williams took over in 1954. Continued as a Dairy run by Mr. and Mrs. Clive Remnant from about 1986. this is still called HIGH STREET DAIRY.

126.	Mr. J. MORTIMORE, Boot and Shoe about 1857- 1890s. Next here may have been the Misses Watts; Dresses and shoes in 1910. Then REES, Hugh Maculay, Draper, date about 1914 - 1923, Haberdashery shop. Then Miss Ada SQUIRE in 1923, Dress and Gown shop. HELENE (Mr. Austin) 1935. Miss H. A. Sanders 1937, by 1945 IRISH LINEN Co. to 1956. Premises up for auction in October 1956. G. F. SWINSONS, Ladies Fashions was the next shop here, the shop was run by Mr. and Mrs E. Mason from about 1976 into the 1980s. They found the old shop sign "Squire" in gold leaf backing when repairs were carried out to their shop sign, Swinsons [17]. It closed down end of 1996 and the shop remained closed for several months. In 1998 Mr. Williams open the shop as D. T. C., COMPUTER CENTRE. Closing in March 2001.

124. A Cycle shop. Mr. SMITH before Mr. William Watts, Boot Maker. Mrs. Watts, Costumier in 1910. Claud Martin 1919. The shop fascia board had MARTIN late SMITH on it, and above the shop were two hanging signs, on one an AA badge and SHELL on the other. Change of trade to the BEEHIVE CAFE, sometime around 1940. DAUPHIN HOUSE, Dress and Gowns 1952 to 1982. It then became FREEZERWISE; Frozen Food, run by Mr. Simon Llewellyn Jones in December 1992. FULFORDS, Estate Agents in 1993.

Mrs. Coles

1934

1934

R. W. SAMPSON,
ARCHITECT
AND
SURVEYOR.

TELEPHONE NO. 102.

MANOR OFFICES,
SIDMOUTH,

April 5 1927

Dear Madam,

    Garage Reconstruction &c

Messrs R. W. & J. Skinner state that their Estimate is made up as follows:—

    Garage work £1071 - 0 - 0
    House addition   379 - 0 - 0
    Total   £1450 - 0 - 0

Yours truly
R. W. Sampson
pp WK

Mrs Martin
High St.
Sidmouth

Estimate for work to be carried out on premises

Mrs. Coles

1938

Next down, set back from the road, we have a reference for the Upper High Street, a Mr Bartlett,1852 - 1857. Mr. J. Burgoyne, 1857 – 1893 Whitesmith, Shoeing, a family business for 40 years, must we believe have been here. The next reference is for a Mr. Tweed, Blacksmith in the early 1900s. Then in 1920, a Motor Cycle and Cycle Works. Mr. W. M. Staples Motor Engineer. Then by 1926, Mrs. C. Martin. An estimate from R. W. and J. Skinner and Architect R. W. Sampson, 5th April 1927, showed a garage reconstruction and house alterations for £1450.0.0. This new part became Martin's Garage. EASTERN MOTORS SIDMOUTH Ltd., around 1937. The forecourt to the garage was built on to make a shop on the ground floor, with a flat on the first floor in about 1938. HIGH STREET GARAGE 1950 - 1960s. The next trade which we have been able to find for the shop is Merryfields Tyres and Batteries in the 1970s. SIDMOUTH TYRE SERVICE, 1988. Then to COUNTRY KITCHEN and BATHROOMS, 1984. HOME STYLE KITCHEN and DECOR to October 1986. Then taken over by Fulfords with their shop next door.

120.   This was the garage. and became Sovereign Cleaners. In December 1990 was converted into a showroom. Opened as SIDMOUTH BED CENTRE.

At the back of the building for a time was Fords work shops. This became No. 122, Willow Picture Framing opening in January 1977.

The small side road to the back of Myrtle Terrace leads to various garages and outbuildings. No 116, Barrett & Gigg, moved here from Selley's Yard. Fords Workshop, Ken Stone, Upholsterer. Number 132, Sidmouth Garage for a short time. Mr. P. Eley had an auction room, now rebuilt as town houses.

Back on to the High Street.

112   Myrtle House was once the property of G. Manning. The building was pulled down in 1889. The site was rebuilt with a red and white brick building with two upper floors to become The Perseverance No. 164 MASONIC HALL in 1890. At the back of the building was the caretaker's cottage.

Sidmouth Museum

Masonic Hall and Myrtle Terrace

MYRTLE TERRACE. A row of seven red brick terraced houses with small front gardens, low brick wall and garden gates. Most of these were advertised as Apartments in the 1920s. All to be changed into shops on the ground floor. The first to change in the 1950s was No.1 then 5, 4, 3, 2, 6 and lastly No. 7. They all had the front gardens built on to make single storey shops.

(No 1) 110 Opened as a Bookshop. L. and J. Copper, The MERMAID Bookshop, closing in May 1992. In September 1993 David Hodgkins opened as SIDMOUTH CYCLES.

(2) 108 SEAGULL, Launderette 1968 to 1985. HIGGINSON & MOORE office, Chartered Accountants. BRADFORD and BINGLEY Building Society 1986. SWINTON, Insurance November 1990. HILL HOUSE HAMMOND 1994.

(3) 106 PETS & GARDENS 1961 to October 1991. Mr. ROGERS, Greengrocer in June 1992 to 1995. The shop then changed to C.M.L. the Office of the SIDMOUTH HERALD.

(4) 104 In 1926 a Mr. Leask was a Grocer and receiver for the Devon and Exeter Savings Bank. Later to become LEASK'S, Painters and Decorators. The shop sold paint, glass, artist materials until 1973. Mr. Roy Bottomley took the shop over, closing down in 1982. Change to office of EVERY and PHILLIPS, Solicitors in January 1983, having moved from Salcombe Road. In May 2001. EVERY PHILLIPS LINFORD BROWNS, SOLICITORS.

(5) 100. Western House. Purnell Daniell Morrell Estate Agents in 1955 and taken over by PETER ELEY.

(6) 98 This was still a house up to the late 1960s. Mr. H. C. Price, Printers, with their shop further down the road, see No 74. Taken over by PETER ELEY; Estate Agents.

(7) 96 Myrtle House. As a house or shop, was occupied by the Pidsley family, Coal Merchants, Milliners, Estate Agents and Builders. We have dates for 1866 to 1902 for this site. Later dates show them in Fore Street. Next date is for MOLLY'S Hair Styles from the 1930s. Under new ownership, it became The HAIR LOFT in July 1993.

94. Mr. and Mrs. F. H. NORTH, Grocers, 1923. Things of Beauty in 1947. Cameo Beauty Parlour mid 1960s. Both by the Tedbury Family. It then changed to BELLS, Shoe Shop in 1962, closing down in February 1998.

Sidmouth Museum

High Street

New name and trade in June 1998, OASIZ, Ladies Fashions. Closing down in August 2000. TAPPERS TRAVEL September 2001, on moving from number 48 High Street.

82.	The site between the shops was built as another shop. This is one of the few new buildings to be built in the High Street. It does not match the existing neighbouring buildings. Mr. Josef POSTA, Jeweller moved here from the Grand Cinema, following the fire that destroyed the building. There was a display window on the side of Carter's shop facing up the High Street which looked part of the shop. Mr Posta retired and closed in November 1981. In August 1982 it became HAWKINS Racing, Bookmakers, and later it became VICKERS. In May 1999 STANLEY RACING.

Mrs. Carter

High Street about 1961

Part of an early Post Card

High Street

80.   The next building was set out nearer the road with a narrow pavement. It used to have on the ground floor a side window looking up the road. The first floor had large bay windows, over the two shops. We have found the following references, but we have not been able to accurately locate the exact positions of their premises, Mr. Joseph Ware, Grocers, with dates of 1856 and 1881. Mr. Harding, with dates 1893 and 1906. Then the name HOUGHTON'S, Sweet Shop, which was taken over by Mr. Birchmore, Grocer in April 1919. We also find the name, Mr. W. F. Down, Groceries. He had another shop in New Street in the early 1900s and a warehouse in Holmdale. We also have a reference for Worth's Grocer, 1925. The shop here in 1929 was MAYFAIR, Ladies Outfitters, Mrs. W. Daniels in 1938, Miss H, Feaken, Proprietress. By 1940 as two shops Mayfair Ladies Outfitters and Mayfair Ladies Hairdressing, Mrs. Ribbons. In the 1940s the left side changed to Children's Outfitters, Miss Borge. By 1960 it changed to G. B. CARTER, Upholsterer and Furnishings. Both traded until February 1969. The building was then demolished, the pavement was widened, and the new building was built back in line with Myrtle Terrace. In February 1971 the new building opened as a Supermarket, RICHWAYS, Upward and Richways Ltd. Later the name change to GATEWAY, and in April 1996 to SOMERFIELD.

76   William Henry Underdown, Fruiterer and Greengrocer and agent for Sutton and Co., Carriers in 1906. By 1919 he had moved to Temple Street. The next reference is for Mrs. Manley, and we have dates of 1926 and 1931. Connie Butters, Confectioner and Tobacconist 1933, Mrs. C. A. Waglyn 1937 to 1960. The premises changed to CHURCHILL'S Cycle shop, trading until November 1987. The business changed in October 1988, Wendy Driver when it became SCARLETTS, Fashion Boutique, until February 1993 when they moved to Church Street. The premises were empty until August 1997, when LUNN-POLY incorporated the premises into their shop next door.

Darlington House

74.   JOHN DOYLE, The Sidmouth Bazaar by 1901. Mr. H. J. PRICE and SON, Toys, Stationers, 1906. The Observer Office moved here from Russell Street in 1908. The Observer

was first published by Miss Letharby as a four-page sheet in 1907, the business was still trading there in 1952. The shop then changed to a Confectioner, Mrs. Connie BUTTERS. She was followed by Mrs. A. TAPLEY, Pottery, Fancy Goods, etc. At the back of the shop, Mr. Tapley sold Auto Cycles. Next the premises changed to The STABLE DOOR, Home Boutique. A. F. Ruplin, in the mid 1960s, before moving to Church Street. Then a change to SIDMOUTH TRAVEL, Mr. Bill Shapland. In the 1980s it became RENWICKS Travel, and then, LUNN POLY, Travel Agents in August 1984.

In shops numbers 74 and 72 they still have the ground floor on split levels, with three or four steps up to the back of the shop.

72. A. W. ELLIS, The Studio, Photographer, in 1901. Mr. Ellis started the first Picture House (Cinema) in Sidmouth in the Drill Hall. On the wall on the Holmdale side there was a large Poster Board advertising the current film on at the Cinema until Mr. Ellis closed the shop. The next trade here was The BANDBOX, Children's clothes in the 1960s. This was followed by BEACHCOMBER in December 1982, Sports wear, and Scandinavian Knitwear. Then CHOICES in 1989, Ladies' Fashions. March 1998 it became a charity shop, CATS PROTECTION LEAGUE.

1907

The Summerland by the Sea   Town Guide

1922   *High Street*

After the turning for Holmdale we come to the only thatched shop left in the town.

70.   Thatched House, at one time called Ethel House. Mrs. C. SLADE had a sweet shop, in 1880. At the back of the shop with an entrance from Holmdale was a yard for the pony and traps that were for Hire etc. Later to become Spencer's Garage. A reference for a Mr. Spencer, Bath Chair proprietor dates 1893 - 1897. Mrs. C. SLADE who in 1902 advertised 'Tyred Carriages for Hire'. Also the Victoria Sanitary Laundry and Depot, Manageress, Clara Slade. By 1935 it had become a Laundry Receiving Office, SIDMOUTH STEAM LAUNDRY. The Laundry was in Sidford, and was run by Mr. Stan Leonard. It was taken over by Mr. Hargreaves of the VICTORIA LAUNDRY (also of Sidford) the shop closed in June 1983. It then became an Antique shop in April 1984. Then FOX'S Antiques to March 1988, when trade changed to The BULB SHOP, Electric fittings etc. In February 1994

it became J. K. L. Video and TV, Electrical goods, closing in September 1998. Reopened in October 1998 as Cardigan House with their other shop also in the High Street. Closed in October 1999. In June 2000 a new trader opened as SANDAL'S.

64   Mr. Jacob 'Stumper' WOOD, Wicker furniture and basket shop here in 1893. The front door next to the shop had a flat roofed porch on ornate iron brackets. By 1919 he had moved to 119 High Street. Next Harry Holland, Fried Fish Dealer by 1923, and in 1930 it had become, EASTMANS, Butchers. DEWHURST, Butchers, 1980s closing December 1999. Empty until October 2000 when, MILLER, Estate Agents, moved from number 83 High Street and opened here.

Post Card

High Street at the top of Holmdale

60   On the corner into Mill Street. This shop front had all small panes of glass, four high and five wide, later to be changed to large plate glass windows. There was a Clode family in Sidbury who were Bakers in 1851. This may be the same family who had this shop as Edwin CLODE, Baker and Grocers in 1878, later run by two Clode sisters, Baker and Grocers, to about 1927. The next name is F. J. BROUGHTON, Confectioner, he won a Gold Medal for bread at Plymouth in March 1931. VINNICOMBES in May 1983.

Cross over the turning to Mill Street, on the corner there were three shops until 1971, when the premises were for sale. On the first floor above the shops, from about 1844 to 1878 there was a Young Ladies' Day School with the names Miss Drusilla Harding and Miss Tighe.

The three shops:

56   Mr. P. Hayman, Ironmonger, in 1828, who also had a workshop in Mill Street. John and Charles, both plumbers 1851. Stephen Hayman, Plumber in 1851. He died in October 1869 and his wife carried on the business. In March 1875 the houses, cottages and workshop were up for sale, and sold to the Haymans for £1,320. About 1914 a Mr. W. H. OLIVER was here, still trading as an Ironmongers and garden tools. Mr. C. Doney 1934, and in 1948 E. W. Rowe, Ironmongers. This shop was built on several different levels, following the slope of the road, (Mill Street), the customers had to go up and down several flights of stairs to complete their purchases.

J. Ankins

High Street at the top of Mill Street

54.   We have a reference for a Mr. William Poole, Ironmonger in 1880, the business to be continued by S. A. and A. E. Poole in January 1891. The next reference is for a Mr. Harry Hindle. Stationers and Tobacconist early 1930 - 1931. Mr. Poole in 1935 - 1939. R. C. Harper, Newspapers and Sweets in the 1940s - 1950s, and Newman in 1970.

52   EVELEIGH Brothers; Antiques, in early 1920s. H. Eveleigh, SIDMOUTH RADIO SERVICE. Customers used to take in their accumulators to be charged up overnight. Mr. Eveleigh also ran a loud speaker set-up for out door events, he put loud speakers on top of his small van and a record player in the back for the old 78s. In 1968 became a fruit shop until 1971.

These three shops were demolished in 1972 and the site rebuilt for The NATIONAL WESTMINSTER BANK. Now called NAT WEST.

Sidmouth Guide and Souvenir

G. M. Thomson & Co.
(Late ARNOLD & HYDE)

AUCTIONEERS, SURVEYORS, VALUERS, HOUSE & ESTATE AGENTS

Principal Agents for
All Classes of Property for Sale or to be Let in Sidmouth and East Devon.
VALUATIONS AND SURVEYS MADE FOR ALL PURPOSES
ESTATES MANAGED
RENTS COLLECTED
MORTGAGES ARRANGED

ALBION HOUSE, HIGH STREET
SIDMOUTH
Tel. 354   Tel. 354

YOUR REQUIREMENTS.—Full particulars of available Properties will be gladly submitted if intending residents will outline the nature of their requirements, stating whether a furnished or unfurnished house, or business premises, etc., is required. Enquiries will be promptly dealt with without fee or obligation.

Local Agents for the "HOMEFINDER" and "COUNTRYSIDE ASSOCIATION."

1932

---

52 High Street

Durham House.
In 1883 it was The C.A.W.G. (Christian Alliance of Women and Girls), continuing to the late 1930s. Miss Acramen was Honorary Secretary in the late 1890s and at a later date, Miss M. A. Haddon. Miss J. M. Pye was Treasurer in the 1930s. Later it became the Y.W.C.A. By 1939 it had changed to a shop. Mr. and Mrs. E. Broughton, a Gentlemen's Outfitters in 1939 to 1968. Also have the name; Mr. R. N. Sandall here in 1952 to 1968. Then a change to a Jewellers shop, KENDALL-TORRY. In March 1987 it became FABRICS and INTERIORS and in August 1991 to 'CARDS &'. Then it became CARDS and NEWS.

Above the shops was a residential flat, which became offices in 1978. Burra Tompson and Co., Thompson Jenner, Accounts.

48   In 1851 Mr. Beaves, Painter and Glazier may have lived here before the ground floor changed into a shop. By 1902 this was a Butchers, Mr. J. H. Barter. Then in 1910 Mr. Parsons. T. W. Dymond, 1914 into the 1930s Then a change of trade, The SKINNER family, Confectionery, they were also Coal Merchants and Agents for rail travel. Then called SKINNERS TRAVEL AGENCY. The Confectionery side closed in 1973. Changed in 1998 to TAPPERS TRAVEL until they moved to number 94 High Street in September 2001.

44.   Clovelly House. Mr and Mrs H. S. Potbury were there in 1895, and the properties remained in the ownership of the Potbury family into the 1950s, when they still had their early phone number; No.14. One of the buildings that has hardly changed on the Street Side. It later became a guest house and in April 1983 CLOVELLY TEA SHOPPE, Mr. and Mrs. Weedon, and to CLOVELLY COFFEE HOUSE and Restaurant February 1994, Roy and June Perry.

As this is the first coffee house we have reached there may be time for a coffee here or at Sue's Pantry a little way down the road.

40.   Coniston House. In 1850, Mr. H. M. Sellek, Paperhanger. By 1893 the property was a shop, Miss Biffen, Milliner to 1907. Mr. Reginald Tucker, Music Shop, 1910. Sellek and Son, Painters, 1919. In August 1931 demolition of the old building. A new building was built by Barnard and Co. to become Bank House, BARCLAYS BANK.

38   Kent House. Mr. E. Bowden, Grocers in 1868, also Agents for Gilbey Wines. In July 1879, Mr. Bowden was assigned to trustee instead of liquidation or bankruptcy. In August Mr. T. Channon, Bowden's manager bought the business. In 1883, also Receivers of Deposits for the Devon & Exeter Savings Bank. We have found the following dates for the Channon family:- William, Farmer/Dairyman 1850 - 1857. Alexander, Printer and Bookmaker, Market Place 1866 - 1870, and in Old Fore Street in 1878 - 1889. Theophilus, Grocer, Tea and Provisions in the High Street 1890 -1919. In 1925 J. LEASK, Grocer, also receiver for the Devon and Exeter Savings Bank. Next in 1939, SANTER & SON, Provision Merchants and Bacon Specialists until 1968 when in December J. BRUNT Ltd. took over opened as a Wine and Spirits shop, Alistair Hay, Manager to 1973. Next, a change of trade, Teenage Clothing, trading as PEPPA until January 1982. Then became FEATHERS, to 1986. New name QUILLS in November 1987. Different trade in May 1991, book shop, PARAGON BOOKS, Mr. M. Chapman.

J. Ankins

Santer and Sons

36   Albion House.

A Doctor's and Solicitor's house. Rev. H. M. Lower, 1850. Rev. T. G. Teggin, 1876. Dr. Pullin, 1878. Then it became Solicitors, Radford and Orchard 1902. Arnold and Hyde Solicitors 1920, then becoming G. M. Thomson and Co. Estate Agents in 1932, Next C. S. Mossop. In the 1940s Thomas, Mossop and Mossop. Then Mossop and Whitham 1970s.

34   In 1893 we have a reference for William James Solman, The East Devon Boot Store until 1898, was probably here. In July 1898 F. Rammell, Tailor, Habit and Breeches maker. Mr. Philip Artemas Cottle, Fancy Draper, Ladies Outfitter in 1914. By 1930 it was Potbury and Son, Estate Agents. After them it became part of the Solicitors Mossop and Whitham 1970.

30   Warwick House.

Part as house and shop. 1900 shop section with bay window onto the pavement. Altered into two shops in 1914. House side:- Clode Apartments 1851, Mr James Clode, Painter and Glazier. Mrs Price Daily, about 1862 -1864. Dr. and Mrs. Pullin in the mid 1870s. Solicitors, R. N. Chard 1930s to mid 1940s. Chard and Coxwell to the 1950s. Ford Simey and Ford from the mid 1960s. Now Ford Simey Daw Roberts. In 2001 changing to Hugh James Ford Simey.

1898, Outside Albion House and number 34

G. Dean

Dean's Bakers. Now a Solicitors Office

The next shop (no Number) was HOSKINS and Son, Bakers in 1902. This was partly rebuilt with a new shop front, made and fitted by Sanders of Old Fore Street. We also have the date 1917 for J. O'DONOGHUE, Antiques. In 1923 Harry DEAN, Confectioner. The Bakery was in Temple Street. (Tel 8). In the 1950s, Mr. and Mrs. P. Dean had the Tudor Rose Restaurant. The shop changed to Chubb Bakeries Ltd.1968. The SHELL SHOP, 1980s and changed to ALL SEASONS in 1987. Later to be taken in to Ford Simey Daw Roberts, Solicitors (30). In 1970s Part of building next to Woolworths was a Tea room. In 1974 George Hardy, TUDOR ROSE Restaurant, In December 1981 Mr. Hardy was granted a Liquor Licence, and so premises became TUDOR ROSE BAR and RESTAURANT. Closed in January 1996 for a short time, now open again as the TUDOR ROSE. In April 1998 new owner, Mr. Mark Thompson.

THE HAYES a large house with five windows on first floor. On the ground floor, two windows either side of the front door with a pillared porch on two columns, onto the pavement, post and chains around a narrow cobbled fore court. Dr. Cohen. Dr. Thomas here in 1850. Later Dr. Bird, Dr. Grant Wilson in the 1920s. The house was demolished for a new store, F. W. WOOLWORTH & Co. Ltd, which opened on 12th. August 1938. The 3d and 6d Stores. Now just called WOOLWORTHS.

16. Next door was Hayes Cottage, or Old Hayes. Thomas Hodge, 1830. Dr. Benjamin Hodge to 1883. Mr. and Mrs. Faulkner 1895. Dr. Macindoe 1902. In 1937 For Sale. In the last war the army had a gun emplacement built out into the road, and barracks in the house. In 1948 all the ground floor was rebuilt with a new shop front, HAYES STUDIO, Mr. H. Fish, Photographer, to 1974. Change of trade, to a Building Society, the ALLIANCE, and then became THE ALLIANCE and LEICESTER. They moved to Fore Street in 1993. Then a different trade again, as Confectioners, SUE'S PANTRY opened in 1993.

J. Ankins

September 1987

14.	(4)	Eaton House. James HOOK, Butcher in 1851. SELLEK Butcher until 1876 when H. Bolt took over. In August 1878 the shop and dwelling house, slaughter house and yard were for sale by the owner Mr. W. Sellek, living in London. It became F. HOLMES, butchers, keeping the name to April 1987, when TILE and PINE, Pat and Alan Parish, opened their shop in addition to their existing Mill Street premises.

12.	(3a)	Misses A. B. & M. HAWKINGS, Costumiers, in 1930 - 1950s. The television cable firm, called VIEWLINE opened until 1975, they built a TV receiving mast on Muttersmoor on Peak Hill and ran cables all over Sidmouth. It seemed as if nearly every house or garden had a cable on or around it. Then SUNTREND, Sunblinds. CHARACTER COTTAGES Self catering holidays. Followed by SUE WILDE in May 1981, Costume hire. In 1989 TILE and PINE combined with their shop next door (14) making one large shop.

J. Ankins

1982, Lennards and S.W.E.B.

10.   (3) A private three storey house. Mr. Samuel and Abigail Chick, Lace Dealer, came to Sidmouth in 1849 and moved into Castle House, High Street. Samuel Chick and his wife Harriet moved here by 1851 staying to 1897. He may have had a sale room or small shop on the ground floor. The main part was at the back with an entrance in Russell Street, with the workshop on the first floor reached by an outside stairway. They made their own lace employing local people, and buying in from lacemakers working in their own homes around Sidmouth. The first name as a shop was HEDGES BROS. Shoes (hanging sign, K Shoes) to about 1918. Then Frederick George STEGGERS, Boots and Shoes. By 1929 LENNARDS Ltd., Footwear here until March 1982. The next trade, Jewellers; SHIPTON and Co.

Frith & Co. Post Card

1913

Over the shops numbers 4, 3, 2, 1 were various offices or work rooms over the years.

2   Mr. R. PASSMORE (Established 1867) Watchmaker. Trading here in 1881. He bought the shop, outbuildings and yard in 1902 for £710, the shop had a large double-sided clock hanging over the pavement, which was still there in 1932. Trade and name changed to JONES, Fruit and Fish. He had the first stainless steel shop front in Sidmouth. In 1936 The EAST DEVON ELECTRICITY BOARD moved their Office and Showrooms from Church Street. Later became SOUTH WESTERN ELECTRICITY BOARD. Then S.W.E.B. The showroom side closed in 1992, and the rest closed in 1994.

In June 1995 LENTONS moved here from Fore Street, Ladies and Menswear. Closed down in October 1998. In early 1999 following a new shop front and alterations, the premises opened on February 17th as THE OLIVE GROVE, Delicatessen, Coffee House and Bistro.

1.   The first reference which we have is for a shop on the corner with Russell Street. In 1887, DAY BROTHERS, Booksellers, Printers and Publishers of the first Sidmouth Observer. It was owned by H. Burnall Day, who first produced a four-page news sheet, which was later extended to eight pages. In 1889, it was relinquished to Mr. H. J. Price, He moved to 74 High Street by 1906. In 1910 the shop was DAY and BATH, this included, East Devon Books Ltd., a Religious Tract Society Depot and Library, also pianos and toys. The business name remained as Day and Bath until 1949 when the premises changed to WYMANS, Booksellers and to MENZIES, Stationers in the 1970s. A new trade, Ian WINCHESTER'S Greengrocer in 1973. Later became IAN WINCHESTER & SONS.

Sidmouth Museum

1954

HIGH STREET, WEST SIDE

Continuing our walk, we will cross over the road and work are way back up the High Street.

We have several references for Mrs. Biffen, Art Needlework and Fancy Draper. An advert in the Sidmouth Observer is linked to the name Macdermid. The business passed to Bathurst and Hayward in 1892. An advertisement for Mrs. Biffen's shop in December 1893 said 'High Street' but no name or number for the shop given. In a guide book of 1907 Mrs. Biffen was still advertising her shop, but still no address was given, on the back of an old photograph of the shop, a hand written note stated, 'Opposite the Devon and Cornwall Bank', (Lloyds TSB now) This must have been were Barclays Bank is now.

From an Old Photograph   *Mates Guide*

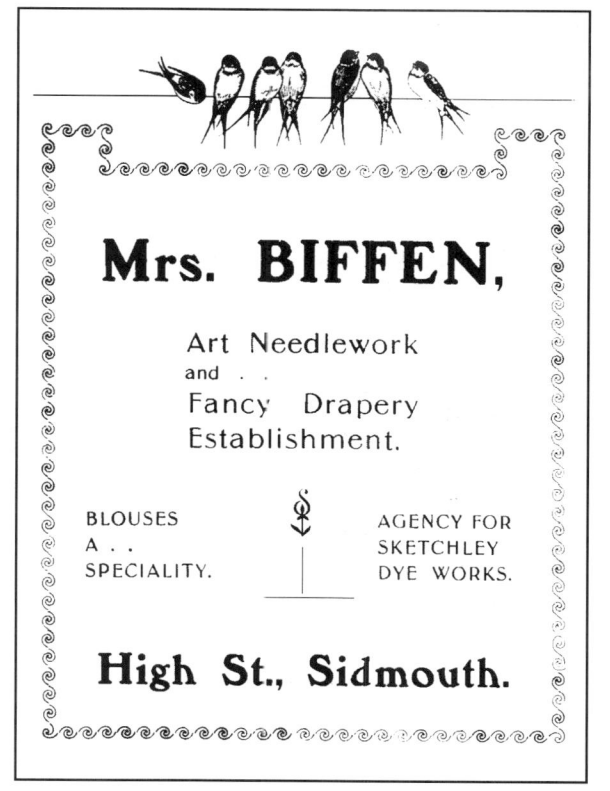

7th December, 1892   *1907*

Bristol House.

(No. 1) Starkey and Knight Old Brewery and Wine shop. The first date, which we have is 1868, also the names, Ford Thomas and Son 1893, and George Brake, Wine and Spirit Merchant, and may have been here. We have the name, A. Channon, Bookseller, 1883-1878. In 1897 the name Alfred J. Davis, Draper. He had moved to Old Fore Street by 1902. By 1919, E. MACDERMID'S Ltd. General Drapers. Early telephone number No.10. Mr. W. A. Caldwell continued trading under the name of Macdermid's Ltd. In the 1950s it changed to The INTERNATIONAL STORES. General Grocers until they closed down in January 1984.

Observer and General Advertiser

TOWN BREWERY, SIDMOUTH.
GEORGE BRAKE,
WINE AND SPIRIT MERCHANT,
BEER, ALE & PORTER BREWER.
Superior Pale and Bitter Ales.
Families supplied in Casks from 5 Gallons upwards.

1868/69

Sidmouth Museum

The next change was alterations to convert the premises into two shops, number 3 and 5.

3.   K SHOES, opened in November 1985. Changing to CLARKS in 2000.

5.   SECONDS OUT, clothes shop April 1985. Then JAYMAX. Then IMPRESSIONS in 1987. SECOND THOUGHTS, clothes shop 1989. Next name change to RICHLEYS. In February 2000, QS. Clothes shop.

Milton House

This was one big shop with a large front door in the centre. G. R. CLARKE, Picture framer and fine arts, there in 1841. Then in 1903, SAMUELS, they were still here in 1910. Next date 1919 Harold PRESTON, Photographer, and Art Gallery, Picture frame maker. Followed by Mr. Coker, Arts and Crafts about 1935-1939. Florence Upton, Fancy and Leather Goods mid 1940s.

This shop in turn was made into two shops, Numbers 7 and 9. Milton House.

7.   Mr. L. Shephard (Fareham) Ltd. in 1949. Mr. C. Hockin, followed by Mr. G. Cooper in 1968. COOPERS of Sidmouth, Mens Clothes. By 1987 it had changed to STAG, Menswear.

9.   Leslie N. Lee, Sports Equipment in the mid 1950s. LEATHER and TRAVEL GOODS. By 1968 Mr. Bernard Hood, Proprietor. Leather and Travel Goods and Greeting Cards. FEATHERS in 1987, Clothes Shop.

11.   Next to the shops were two thatched cottages, which were there before 1841, filling all the space from Preston's shop to Potburys. The cottage site was rebuilt about 1850. A large tall red brick building, called Rahere House, which was the home and surgery of Dr. Bingley Pullin, until 1919. At sometime, (date unknown) the left side of the building on the ground floor was made into a shop, H. R. REES, Dresses, was here in 1897 to about 1917 when it changed to WORLDS STORES, Grocers, The premises changed to KNEELS Dry Cleaning in the 1960s, adding shoe repairs and key cutting later. In August 1998 renamed JOHNSONS.

The rest of the house was made into the NATIONAL PROVINCIAL UNION BANK

Potbury's on the right

in 1919. By 1926 NATIONAL PROVINCIAL BANK. In October 1977 S.E.S. (Services Equipment and Supplies), moved from Old Fore Street , making the ground floor into a shop.

M. Davies

Charlie Davis, Bert Payne, Jim Harris, 1934

    Next door was the site of the Poor House, which was built in the late 1580s and John Arthurs, Alms house 1705. Part of this site was exchanged for a site in Mill Street when a new poor house was built in 1802 near the river, this allowed John Arthur to extend his house in the High Street. Mr. Richard Farrant, Auctioneers, 1830. Rebuilt in 1849 by Charles Farrant. Trading for a number of years as C. Farrant, Furnishings. The Farrant's also traded in Timber, Slate, Coal Merchants and Estate Agents.

Arthur House.
25.   John Potbury. After Charles Farrant died in the 1861 it became POTBURY and SONS, Furnishers, Auctioneers. Tel. 14. Remained in the Potbury family into the mid 1970s. Mrs. E. Potbury died in 1974. Her husband had died in 1955. The firm was run by directors, Mr. Roy Blake, Mr. F Howe and Mr. T. Lee. The business is still run by directors under the name of POTBURYS.

Potbury & Sons,

CABINET MAKERS AND UPHOLSTERERS.

Removal Contractors,

FURNITURE AND LUGGAGE WAREHOUSED.

Auctioneers, House and Estate Agents.

Lists of Houses to be Let Furnished or Unfurnished sent on application.

APARTMENTS SECURED.

VALUATIONS MADE.

INVENTORIES TAKEN OR CHECKED.

1894

Ladysmith House.

Originally a house with small gable porch over the central front door, with steps down to the pavement. Iron railings out to the pavement in front of bow windows. Then made into two shops on the ground floor. The outside of the building, above the front shop is interesting. The brick wall is not in a straight line, the left side goes in at a angle, then straight and back at an angle, whilst the facia board and guttering are straight. Mr. J. Woodley to G. Bartlett in March 1877. Mr. E. T. Sellek in September 1878. In 1885 the dwelling house and shop were for sale, but they did not reach the reserve price of £395. After this it became SELLEK, Ironmongers. This was a real old fashioned Ironmongers, one could buy just what one wanted, if one wanted five screws of different size, that is what one got. The shop remained with the Sellek family to October 1970. There were nearly always large advertising signs on the wall between the first floor windows over the shop door. It then changed to LADYSMITH HOUSE, Antiques, which was run by Miss D. Kirkham and Miss Hilda Jones, until it became POTBURY'S, Estate Agents in 1983. In 1996 this shop was combined with the shop next door (number 33). The shop doorway was taken out and replaced by a window. It is now called POTBURYS.

Mr. Sellek

High Street. 1930 - 1932

33.   GAITE and BERWICK, Milliner, in April 1901. We have the name Miss A. Davies, Fancy Drapers for 1930. W. A. GILBERT, Milliner to 1947. Mrs. Slade closing in 1971. Hilda Jones, Antiques. Objets d'Art in the 1980s. Changed to Ladysmith House by 1989. In 1996, POTBURYS.

Osborne House.
39.   This was a large two storey house, with a small gable porch over a central front door and step down to the pavement. In 1850 Mr. Harding and Family. Mrs. D. Harding, Dressmaker, Scotch yarn sock maker, 1870. Mr. Charles Harding, Watchmaker, Miss Harding had a Day School about 1878 - 1893 for young Ladies. We also have the name Mrs. Sellek, and we believe she may have run the school with Miss Harding, have the dates, 1872 and 1876. We think the school may have been on the first floor of the building, The house owned by J Potbury was sold to The Devon and Cornwall Bank in 1888, having moved from 2 York Terrace where it had been since March 8th 1886. All the front and ground floor was rebuilt. It then changed to LLOYDS BANK, who purchased the building in 1906 and the entire front was rebuilt as it is today. In July 1999, Lloyds TSB.

Mitchell's Cycle Shop

Honiton House.

    We have not been able to find when this house was changed to a shop. At the back of the building there was a Glove Factory in 1880. The names, Mitchell and Woodward 1889-1890. Mr. Frederick Mitchell in 1893-1897, Driving Glove and Gaiter Maker. We also have the names: E. Kemphorne, F. H. Porter, N. G. Barte, 1907.
In 1902 it was one shop, Mr. Frederick Mitchell, The SID VALE CYCLE DEPOT, he had a workshop at the back, leading onto Church Lane. In 1912, Mr. Elliot and Rose Breach had the shop, Wireless Supplies. They were the only agent for H M V Records in Sidmouth. They had the first wireless sets in the town for sale. A. G. Hayward, 1913. We also have the name F B Wright, Gramophone shop for 1930-1931. Which must have been here. In March 1946 the business changed to Michael Hayklan, Furrier. In 1944 or 1946 the shop changed into two units, the central doorway was converted into two doors, which were set at an angle inside the shopfront. So we now have numbers 45 and 46. Mr Burgoyne as the owner.

45.   M. HAYKLAN, Furrier, 1946. Elizabeth Cochrane, Furrier, 1949. Mr. Burgoyne sold out to PETER MARSH, Bespoke Tailors. In August 1970 Mr. Desmond Werring, still trading today under the name Peter Marsh.

D. Richards

Sign Board from over the Shop

47.   BURGOYNE'S, Travel Bureau, 1951, and then as Stationers, cards, gifts. Closing in August 1999. In October 1999, Mr. Stiles opened as BYGONE ERA. Antiques, moving to number 123 High Street in November 2001.

Abernethy House.

49.   This building had a narrow front garden with iron railings. There was a bay window on each side of the central front door, and two bay windows on the first floor. Sliding sash windows on the second floor. George Stocker, General Practitioner whose address was Western Town in 1851, may have been here before Dr. Bingley Pullin, 1830, Dr. T. H. Pullin and T. H. Stocker MD., who were here in 1872. In a newspaper cutting dated, October 1911, it stated, 'Dr. Pullin left Abernethy House to his son Stuart with request to neither sell nor change its name'. The premises changed to a Bank in 1912. The ground floor was altered, three new windows were placed in the middle, with new doorways at each end. The alterations were made for The NATIONAL WESTMINSTER BANK. In October 1976 the front of the ground floor was rebuilt, placing the front door back in the centre between a four columned porch with a bay window on each side, for The BRISTOL & WEST Building Society. Part of the building had the offices of Burra and Thompson, Solicitors, in the 1979 - 1980s. Agents for Cheltenham and Gloucester, Building Society. E C S computer supplier in the 1990s.

55.   Two small cottages owned by Mr. W. J. Govier. Tailors in the 1870s. The premises were converted into a shop and opened in the autumn of 1904, as V. J. GOVIER, Glass and China shop, 55 High Street. In 1929 became Govier and Son. Under which name it traded ever since.

Five thatched cottages. Occupied by: McLeod, Shopkeeper 1852, a Greengrocer in Back Street (Old Fore St.), Evens, Shoes, Burroughs, Bishop, and Shepherd, however, we do not have trade references for these three. The cottages sold for £370 in 1882. The site was later rebuilt.

A report in Lethaby's Sidmouth Journal and Directory August 1886, stated that the last of the three awkward corners, at the junction of High Street and Upper High Street had been removed and that the erection of the Wesleyan Chapel, although having a heavy stony frontage, was a welcome improvement. The chief regret being the inability to carry the improvement a few yards further on, taking away the projection of Castle House and so connecting the footpath on the side with that in front of Hillsdon, Mr Wright's private residence.

Wesley House.

A private house. Rev. Noel and J. Chen in 1937. Rev. and Mrs. D. Male in early 1940s, the Rev. C. L. Riches in 1949. Later made into a shop on the ground floor. In February 1955 the name changed to The Steps. Norman Winckworth. Antiques. 1969 THE STEPS, TEA ROOMS. January 1970, JOANNES, Ladies Hairdressers. 1978 Bernard Hulbert, The HAIR STUDIO and later to HAIR and GRACES. Now Geoffrey Hadley, The HAIR STUDIO.

Castle House, and Union Court House.

Castle House.

A private house, Thomas H. Pullin, 1853-1875. C. P. Harris, Private Tutor about 1869-1870 and for a time a Ladies School, which was opened in July 1877 by Miss Davies and Miss Hook. By 1880 only Miss Davies listed in a directory, not as a School.

Castle House became The Town Hall and Council Offices in 1895. The first mention of a Museum, which we have been able to find is 1929, when it was held in the Town Hall, displaying objects of local interest, pictures, lace, and arms of the coastguards[18]. By 1928 the Council Offices had moved to the top of Church Street into Hope Cottage. The site was cleared and The GRAND CINEMA was built and opened in February 1929. The entrance to the Cinema, the box office, foyer, sweet counter and staircase to the balcony were all in the centre of the building. On each side of the entrance were shops, No. 63 and 71. On the first floor was a restaurant, a Ladies Hair Salon, Mr Wallace Beech, with the entrance at the left hand side of the cinema. Mr. Beech had a Hairdressers in the 1930s in Temple Street, he moved here by 1934.

The Cinema was burnt down in 1956. The building was rebuilt, not as a cinema, keeping the old front wall and shop fronts and the large flat iron framed glass canopy over the pavement. In 1991 the large flat iron framed glass canopy, which extended along the full length of the building, over the shop fronts and pavements was taken down. The centre, where the main entrance of the cinema was located, was converted into a shop, and became Number 67, which opened as The CHATTERY, Tea rooms.

M. Baker

Fire in the Grand Cinema, 1956

63.   Left side. Mr. R KIRBY, Soft Furnishings opened in mid 1950s. This became the GRAND STUDIO-FYNART (Devon Ltd.), photographers in 1962. Next R A P, TV sets and line rental. CAMEO in February 1973. TREASURE CHEST, 1977 to August 1987. Next STEPS, FASHION SHOES until May 1991. In June Mr RON CLINT opened a Cycle Shop, which traded until January 1995. In February it changed again, becoming OPTISAVE, Opticians. On February 18th 1999 they closed. In April, BARTLEBY'S, Bookshop, new and secondhand books. In June 2001, renamed BOOK LIFE.

71.   Right hand side. Early 1930s, Confectioner, Mr. Smith. In the 1940s, C. G. COVENTRY OPTICIAN. In 1951, Mr. J. POSTA, Watchmaker, he was born in Czechoslovakia and came to England and joined the Royal Air Force. He was here until the fire in 1956, when he moved to the other side of the road. In September 1960, MILLER and LILLEYS. The premises then became REDFERN and WHITE, Estate Agents and then to REDFERNS, Estate Agents.

Behind the premises in Blackmore Drive, stands the St. John Ambulance Headquarters, built in 1960. On the other side of Blackmore Drive is The Devon County Library and Health Centre, which were opened in June 1970.

Crossing over Blackmore Drive. There was a high brick wall along Blackmore drive and round to the High Street. This was called Blackmore Hall and Estate, the property of Sir John Kennaway. Other later occupants were, Storey, 1815. Lady Miller, mid 1830s. Straham, 1862. Lear, 1868. Fisher, 1880. Scott, 1887. In the 1940s - 1950s The Hon. Mrs Pleydell-Bouverie.

There were also two large houses, Cherry Hayes, and Grinfield House, (now Hillsdon House). The large gardens went back to the footpath, which runs from Blackmore View to Coburg Road. In December 1913 the Council decided to purchase the Blackmoor Hall Estate, which was about five acres, for £4,250. The Sidmouth Observer, dated 24th December 1913 states, 'There is a lovely garden in good order, a substantial well built house, a large field and another piece of land known as Abernethy garden and stables'. In 1953 the gardens were opened to the public, and were called Coronation Gardens. The house was demolished in 1956.

75. The high brick wall was removed and a new building built in 1969. This became The DEVON and EXETER SAVING BANK, having been in Fore Street. It then changed to The T S B (Trustee Savings Bank). Which closed in August 1999 when it became Lloyds TSB. On August 18th 2001, David Stanton opened as SIDMOUTH MOBILITY.

77 and 81. Next up the road, General Grinfield built Grinfield House. This was a large three storey house with a central front entrance, four stone steps up to the front door, a large flat porch roof on round pillars, and narrow garden with railings. In the late 1830-1860s it was owned by a Cutler, who was aptly named Mr. J. Cutler. In 1870 the house became empty. In the Spring of 1872, a Mrs. Brown and a Miss Brophy moved in and the house was renamed 'Hillsdon'. In the 1880s a Doctor and Mrs. Wright were in residence. Then a Dr. and Mrs. Williams, about 1890-1895. Then by a Dr. George A. Leon, 1896 until about 1906, Dr. Colclough, 1910-1919. He was succeeded by Dr. Cohen and Dr. Michelmore. Next came Dr. Fison, HILLSDON SURGERY. The premises then became a Dentist's Surgery, with Mr. M. Wood, Mr Vallender, into the 1960s.

The ground floor was divided up, a shop made on the right-hand side. Number 81. The other side became a shop, number 77, then it became the SIDMOUTH AND DISTRICT ESTATE AGENTS in the 1960s. In January 1974 it became the CELTIC CROSS, and November 1978, the business returned to an Estate Agents, HARRISON and LAVERS. In October 1983 a completely new shop front and doorway was installed. It has now become HARRISON-LAVERS and POTBURY'S.

M. Baker

Early picture of Upper High Street (tall building Hillsdon House)

    Next to Hillsdon were two thatched cottages, before being rebuilt as shops. The first reference which we have found is as a Chemists, W. E. PRATT Ltd. in 1937. This was followed by W. H. JAMES. Chemist who had a new shop front in the 1940s. The business was taken over by J. O. McDONALD in January 1964, and continued into the 1970s. Then became HINTON LAKES. Later Cross and Herbert, Chemist. In August 1990 changed to LLOYDS, Chemists.

83.   Next up the road there was a vacant plot adjacent to the Chemist, this gave access to the backs of the shops. In 1988 this land was built on for a new shop. Number 83. This

was one of the few completely new shop buildings in the town. MANN and Co. Estate Agents opened on 10th October 1988. The business changed to CONSTABLES, who were also estate agents in July 1990. In January 2000 new name MILLER, Estate agent until October 2000 when they moved down the road to number 64. New owners, Abhita Jessamy and Iskaan Arthur Gantinas, opened in December as HEALTHYBITZ, Magnetic Therapy Products. In February 2001 the shop closed when they moved to Banwell House, in Old Fore Street.

Two more thatched cottages until the 1930s when Mr. W. E. Staples built a Garage and a lock up shop. In the shop part, Mr. and Mrs. E. J. Boobyer here in the early 1940s. August 1940 shop to Mr. JAMES, Chemists. In 1949 it all became L. A. Hills garage, Ford Dealer. Part of the showroom was rebuilt in 1969, closing April 1983. In July 1984 there were alterations, in order to make The SIDMOUTH SHOPPING CENTRE, an indoor centre of about 18 small shop units.

97. LLOYD MAUNDER, Butchers, in the late 1930s. MACE, Grocers, to the late 1960s. This was followed by CENTRA STARLINE, Grocers until August 1981, and then became NORTHILLS. Shop for sale in 1982. FOX and SONS, Estate Agents, opened in October1982. This was followed by G. A. PROPERTY Services in 1991. In December 1999 the name changed to YOUR MOVE, Estate Agents. Closed in December 2001.

99 BAKER Bros. Fruiterers and Florists in 1938. COUNTRY KITCHENS opened in December 1982, trading until February 1987. The WINE SELLER, March 1987 to October 1994 when it moved into part of Fords. Next, the premises became The FLOWER BASKET in April 1995. Then the premises were empty until May 1996 when a new business began, PORTRAIT HOUSE, Photographers, closing a few months later. Now called CARDIGAN HOUSE, Ladies Outfitters.

107. At the back of the end shop, through an archway, 1 and 2, Cherry Hayes cottages on the left side of the courtyard, with a new building on the right for a Fire Station, opened in July 1933. The Fire Station was a brick building with eight tall sliding doors and high ceiling to take the fire engine with their ladders on top. Outside on the left of the building is a tall training tower. Over the station there was a three bedroom flat for the Station Officer. Mr. C. Colwill was Captain at the time. One of the fire engines was a Merryweather - Albion Engine, bright red with a wooden ladder. The Fire Service moved to Woolbrook in 1965. It then reverted into private ownership, Mr. Norman Cole kept his vintage cars in here. The fire station part became Number107, High Street. It opened as the OLD FIRE HOUSE ART GALLERY. Next John Weaver converted it into offices, Investment and Insurance Broker. CELTIC CROSS, in November 1987, when they moved from Victoria Road. After this it became EAST DEVON FINANCIAL SERVICES CENTRE. In 1990 changed to HILL HOUSE HAMMOND Ltd. In November 1994 the premises were for sale.

In April 1995 it became SIDMOUTH MOTORING MEMORIES, Museum, which closed in January 1998. It has now become SHOOBRIDGE, Funeral services closing in July 2001.

J. Ankins

Leaving the Old Fire Station, 1957

Back onto the High street, there was a row of three thatched cottages, called Pikes Court. Thomas Evans, Boot and Shoe Maker in 1878, and W. Evans, until he moved to Fore Street in 1885. Pepperell, Macey, Hawkins, Stapleton and Howe, in the late 1890s. A passage-way went through to other cottages at the back. In July 1932 all three buildings were pulled down and the site rebuilt. This then became number 111.

111. The first shop became Sidmouth Urban District Council, Gas Department, opened in 1933. A new Library over the Gas Showrooms to 7th November 1936 when they moved to Hope Cottage, Church Street. The shop became SOUTH WESTERN GAS BOARD. Then it became BRITISH GAS until they closed in August 1994. This was followed by a Charity shop, SUE RYDER, to 1996. New trade Mr. Nick Povey opened as TOPSPORTS, in March 1997.

113   (No.68) In the 1850s William Gosling, SID VALE BAKERY. Robert Prince 1856, John S. PRINCE, 1866, Family Bread and Biscuit Bakers. PRINCE and VINCENT in 1878, into the early 1900s, SID VALE STEAM and HYGIENIC BAKERY and then change of owner, Jasper Daw in 1910. Walter Hammett, 1919. Later Mr. and Mrs. W. A. Newbery, SID VALE BAKERY, in the 1920s. The shop was for sale in 1957. We believe may have been a stationers here called Moors. The next reference which we have found for here is SIDMOUTH ELECTRICS, in the 1960s. In 1968, DISCOUNT, a Grocers. Then SOONSAVE in 1974. Then a different trade SECONDS OUT, Clothes shop, to April 1985 when they moved to 5 High Street. Next GALLERIA to October 1986. Empty for a long time. In January 1988 REFLECTIONS, Gifts, China, Glass etc. closing down in May 1998. In October 1998 BETA-PRINT. Closed in July 2000.

Advertisement 1901

119.   George Gilly, Lodging House Keeper in 1851. Mr. BUTTERS and Son, Pork Butchers in the late 1870s. Mr. Butters replaced the cottage with a shop. Mr. WOOD and Sons, Basket Shop, about 1919 to 1948. The IRISH LINEN Co., to 1990. Empty for a time. SUE RYDER charity shop in 1991 to 1992 when BRADLEYS Estate Agents opened in July.

123   This was a cottage occupied by Samuel Cox a Builder in 1851. Mr. J. W. Snell, Men's Hair Cutting about 1889, by 1927 it had become J. W. Snell, Ladies and Gentlemen's High Class Hairdressing Salon. After that E. Abbott, Greengrocers, Flowers in the early 1930s. William Henry SADLER, Watchmaker here in 1938 to the 1940s. change of trade to G. F. SWINSON'S, Ladies Dress and Gowns in the early 1960s. Next CONTINENTAL, Greengrocers, 1980s, to December 1990. Shop empty for a long time.

In October 1992 BETA- PRINTS, Printing and Copy centre until October 1998 when they moved down the road to number 113. October 1999, DRAYCOTT WINES, Colin Bickerstaff, Manager, closing in May 2001 and now BYEGONE ERA, Antiques moved here from number 47 High Street on 1st November.

J. Ankins

1988, Irish Linen

This is the last shop before The Unitarian Chapel and turning into All Saints Road.

FORE STREET, EAST SIDE

We will now go back down the town to where the High Street divides into two roads, Fore Street and Old Fore Street, old names Cheapside and Back Street.

C. Culverwell, Sidmouth Directory

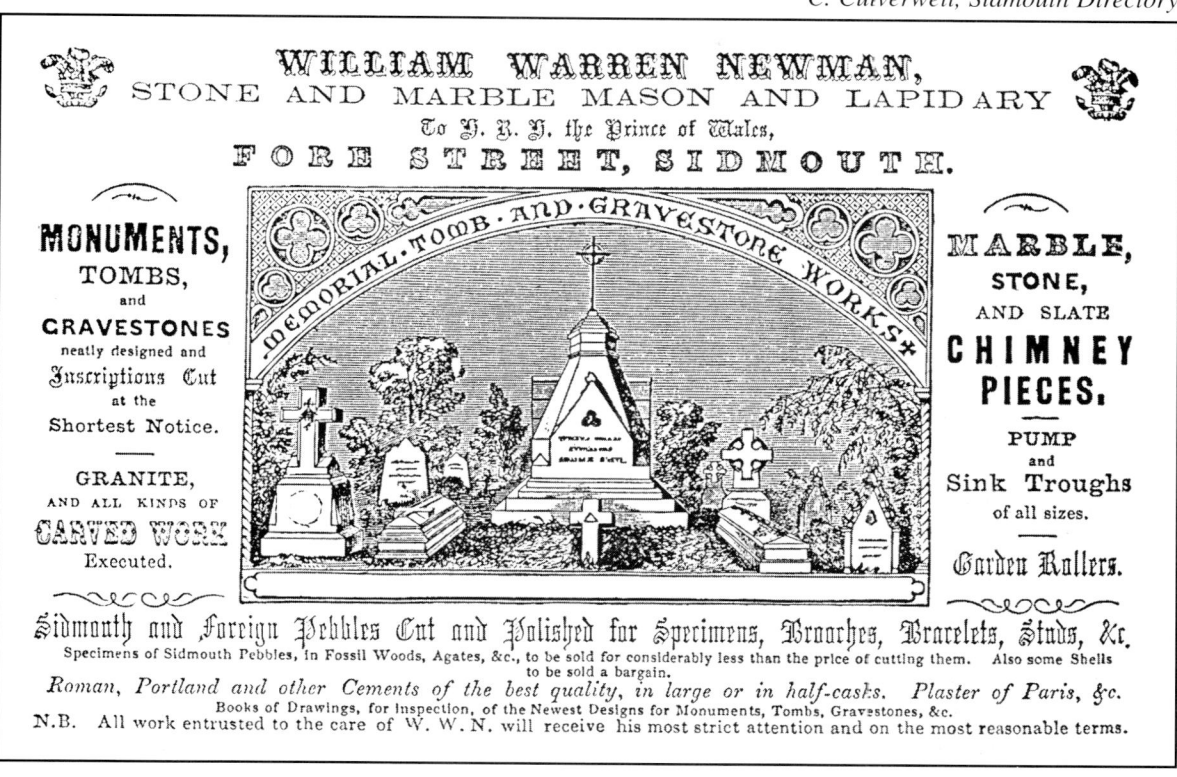

WILLIAM WARREN NEWMAN,
STONE AND MARBLE MASON AND LAPIDARY
To H. R. H. the Prince of Wales,
FORE STREET, SIDMOUTH.

MEMORIAL TOMB AND GRAVESTONE WORKS

MONUMENTS, TOMBS, and **GRAVESTONES** neatly designed and Inscriptions Cut at the Shortest Notice.

GRANITE, AND ALL KINDS OF **CARVED WORK** Executed.

MARBLE, STONE, AND SLATE **CHIMNEY PIECES.** PUMP and Sink Troughs of all sizes.

Garden Rollers.

Sidmouth and Foreign Pebbles Cut and Polished for Specimens, Brooches, Bracelets, Studs, &c.
Specimens of Sidmouth Pebbles, in Fossil Woods, Agates, &c., to be sold for considerably less than the price of cutting them. Also some Shells to be sold a bargain.
Roman, Portland and other Cements of the best quality, in large or in half-casks. Plaster of Paris, &c.
Books of Drawings, for Inspection, of the Newest Designs for Monuments, Tombs, Gravestones, &c.
N.B. All work entrusted to the care of W. W. N. will receive his most strict attention and on the most reasonable terms.

18th September, 1868

The following businesses were in Fore Street, but we have not been able to accurately locate them, Mr John Stone, shopkeeper in 1850, his trade may have been Greengrocer, and Richard a Grocer in the High Street in 1870. Thomas Stone, Carver and Gilder. W. Boon, Shopkeeper, Grocer, in 1852-1857. William Bray, Photographer 1866, in 1890 still advertised in Fore Street.

In 1822 the Sidmouth Directory listed James Newman, Stone Mason. In 1836 Thomas Newman. An advertisement of 1868 showed a William Warren Newman, Stone Mason, in Fore Street, to 1889, but have been unable to find out which premises he occupied. We have also found a reference for William and James Newman in the High Street 1856-1879, and James in Fortfield Road 1867-1902 stone mason and Lapidary. Dingwall, Fruiterer and Florist. 1897, Miss Harriet Dare, shopkeeper, 1923, probably a dress shop. Also in the Pigot

Directory 1830, shopkeepers and dealers in sundries, Robert Pidgeon, Samuel Thorne and Robert Wakeham. Yvonna, Ladies Outfitters in 1935. Ernest J. Staples, Arts and Crafts 1937 and in Old Fore Street in 1939. The Work Box, Miss Edith Taylor, Needlework, wool shop in 1939.

The first building we reach is on the corner with Russell Street, Meredith House. 25, Wellington House No.26. John RUSSELL, Bakers, in 1823. By 1851 Thomas Russell employed three men and his son George. In May 1882 George Russell had the house rebuilt, and in September the business carried on in the new building as G. RUSSELL and SONS. Next it became CONANT'S, Bakers. In the early 1900s it then changed to JIMMY HOSKINS, Bakers. In 1918 the trade changed to Watchmaker and Opticians, Mr. A. J. BOYCE. The family kept the business until 1978 when HODGES took over and made it into a Men's Outfitters. They closed in January 1994. The shop was empty for a time. It had short lets around Christmas time, as JUST A POUND. DAYS GONE BYE, Gift shops, and various gift type shops. Empty again by the end of 1996. More short lets to 1998 when it opened as NEW TOUCH, closing in January 1999. Then became SHAULS, Bakery, Delicatessen and Coffee Shop, opened in July 1999.

Mrs. Mathieson

Miss Boyce's, Shop

Next down the road, the name John Bond, Cordwainer with an apprentice boy in 1851. Probably not a shop until it became THE KANDY SHOP, run by Miss Boyce, Sweets, Tea room and Ice creams. They made their own Ice creams with the ice made in Selleys Yard. This Shop had a very fine shop front made in Mahogany, a large 16 light door set back with a bay window on each side. The shop closed in 1964. All the fine shop front and doorway were taken out and the premises made into HODGES as one large shop.

On down the road, William Saunders, Cabinet maker with four men and an apprentice in 1851. Mr John DYER, Saddle and Harness maker and warehouse man in 1865. In 1868 he opened a new showroom, he gave notice of bankruptcy in July 1878. In August 1879 the shop and dwelling house were for sale. Mr. Jesse (Skipper) FARRANT, had a shop here in 1902, Saddler and Leather worker. FARRANT and Sons in 1926. Next it became J. H. LOOMES, Grocer to the mid 1930s when it became CATHCART & CATHCART Estate agents. Later CATHCART CATHCART and PIKE. The premises became a Building Society, the BRIDGEWATER and then the BIRMINGHAM Building Society, changing to BIRMINGHAM MIDSHIRES, until they closed in September 2000. In May 2001 new trade, JAG Mobile Phones.

Sidmouth News

Outside Whitton's Butcher Shop in Fore Street

22.   We have a reference for 1830, Mr. Frederick Hooke, Butcher and wife Sarah, two Daughters, Elizabeth and Anne, a son James, all born in Sidmouth, here to January 1865

when Mr. W. H. Lloyd took over. This reference overlaps the next dates. John Whitton, started a Butchers business in 1863, a tenant farmer at Boughmore. Mr. S. Wheaton and John Whitton Butchers were here to 1869, when S. Wheaton moved to his own shop in Church Street. Then became, F. J. WHITTON, later WHITTON and SON around 1919. It was known as the 'Fore Street Music Hall'.[18] as often a passer-by would hear songs from Gilbert and Sullivan, or songs from the show of the day. The shop stayed in the Whitton family until 1950. The next date is 4th. February 1950, when it changed to an Ironmongers,
TUCKER and Son and then to F. J. Tuckers HOME CARE Centre about 1970. By 1981 CONSUMER MARKET. 1998 CONSUMER HOUSEWARES.

Sidmouth News

21. Next down, we have the name Henry Porter, Watch and Clock maker in 1851, still here in 1870. The premises then changed to the Tedbury Family. Daniel, Dairyman and Poulterer in 1883, also an agent for the Sutton and Co. parcel carriers. Frank, in 1906, Miss E Tedbury, Dairyman in 1926, Frederick, Dairy shop, 1939. An old picture in the Sidmouth News, published in December 1973 showed the shop taken near Christmas, with the name TEDBURY on a board high up across the first floor window, with ten rows of poultry hanging all over the outside of the shop. In the picture was 'Kidney' Whitton, Butcher Ebdon, Danny and Mrs. Tedbury.
In the 1940s, F. Tedbury, Milkbar, to the 1950s. HOUSE OF TEDBURY in the 1960s. And CAMEO BEAUTY

Tedbury's Milk Bar

PARLOUR. Then a change of trade to LEACROFT GALLERIES, Antiques. Next were THABER Galleries in 1980s, then GALLERY 21, closing in June 1997. In June 1998 opening as a Picture Shop, Sidmouth FINE ARTS, Carol Stoneman.

20. The first name which I have for the next door shop, is Mary 'Granny' Bolt, home made sweets and Greengrocer in 1889, by 1910 she had moved to Old Fore Street. The next name is Mr. Charles E. GREEN, Flower Shop in 1923. This was one of the longest family run shops at the same premises. Closing in 1995. The shop empty for some time before opening as SEDMUDA, Ladies Fashions in May 1997 to September 2000 when they closed.

19. Mr. Frederick Mitchell, Painter and Glazier, from 1851 to the 1870s. As a shop, Miss Brooking, Milliner, Fancy Drapery was here in 1883. Mr. John Trick, Fishmonger in 1890-1893 and Mary in 1897, with John listed as a Certificated Plumber/Gas Fitter. By 1902, John Trick, had a cycle Shop to 1906. Next trade name may have been Risdon, before Beatrice Spencer, a Milliner. GAINSBOROUGH HOUSE Antiques, about 1936. They closed in December 1982. IDEAS in November 1992, Gifts, Knitwear, to December 1986. In February 1987 a charity shop, IMPERIAL CANCER RESEARCH FUND.

J. Ankins

C. Green's, September 1987

18   As a house, Mr. William Potbury mid 1850s. Also the name Samuel Warren, Butcher for 1851. It became a Fish Shop, with wrought iron sign over the shop window, F. PIPER in the late 1880s to about 1902, he had one of the first telephones, No.17. Shop sold to W. (Banty) Hook, also a fish shop. They had their own well for water supply.
Then in the sixties H. SCRATCHLEY, Estate Agent, now part of ALLIANCE and LEICESTER Building Society from February 1992.

Sidmouth Museum

1901, Piper Fish Shop

✠ **M. G. BOND,** ✠
MANUFACTURER & IMPORTER OF EVERY DESCRIPTION OF
LADIES', GENTLEMEN'S, & CHILDREN'S
BOOTS, SHOES, SLIPPERS, GOLOSHES,
FORE STREET, SIDMOUTH.
Agent for Pinet and Meyer, Parisian Manufacturers.
A STAFF OF FIRST-CLASS WORKMEN KEPT.
Registry Office for Servants.

1884

The next shop down the road was M. G. Bond, Boots and Shoes here in 1836 to about 1902. Walter Hawkins "YE OULDE BOOTE SHOPPE." to about 1918, and then Mrs. W. Hawkins, Dress and Gowns to 1926. John HINTON LAKE, Chemist, Telephone number 19. He may have taken over this shop before the shop was amalgamated into the next door shop. It was still HINTON LAKES to February 1992 and now with number 18, ALLIANCE and LEICESTER Building Society.

The Building next door in 1851 was John Holwill, Tailor and Draper. Alterations to the building in 1898 and opened as COLEBERD and Co. Cash Dispensing Chemists by 1897. Changing to Cross and Herbert Ltd. opening as HINTON LAKE and Son Ltd. by 1925. Mr. Garnet Skinner, and then his son, John took over the business. In 1990 it was taken over by LLOYDS Dispensing Chemist. The shop was converted back into two shops, to form part of ALLIANCE and LEICESTER, on the left. The right hand shop LLOYDS, Chemist. 1993 LLOYDS SUPERSAVE DRUGSTORES. Then became HOLLAND AND BARRETT, Health Food shop.

Mates Guide

Ye Oulde Boote Shoppe
(ESTABLISHED A CENTURY).
WALTER HAWKINS

High-class Boot and Shoe Maker.

Agent for PINETS, LION, GLOBE BRANDS, and all the principle makers.

REPAIRS.

Hand-Sewn a Speciality.

FORE STREET, SIDMOUTH.

1907

16   From the mid 1800s this has been a Newsagent and Stationers. JOHN HARVEY Printer and Bookseller, was born in Lyme Regis and his wife, Ann and one Daughter Ann Elizabeth, here 1830. He printed and published, Harvey's Sidmouth Directory. Number 1 in January 1850. price one penny. In 1853 an advertisement in his Directory stated 'The Library containing above 4,000 volumes of the most modern and approved Works'. About 1867, changed to Charles CULVERWELL, Printers and they printed the Sidmouth Advertiser, published fortnightly and the Sidmouth Journal and Directory, published on 3rd and 18th of each month, later weekly. Change of name, E. Culverwell and Son, Stationers. The printing, etc. was done in the back of the shop, entrance in East Street. They were also producers of the first electricity supply to shops in Fore Street. This was produced by a gas engine driving an electricity generator. No date for this can be given but it must have been about the turn of the century. The gas engine was remarkable in that the fly wheel was about 6ft in diameter and

Sidmouth Directory and Advertiser

COLLARD & COLLARD'S PIANO FORTES FOR SALE OR HIRE, At CULVERWELL's Circulating Library.
☞ All NEW MUSIC, either in Stock or to order, at HALF-PRICE.
London Daily Papers supplied at the Published Prices.
Brown Paper for laying under Carpets, &c., 4ft. 6in. in width. Cut to any length. 3d. per Yard.

1868

Harold Fish

1963, Herald Office

started by two men (or a man and boy) turning the fly wheel until the machine fired. Once that happened it would go on running day and night. The hard work was getting the engine started. The gas engine was also used for driving the printing machine for the Herald every Friday. Electric lighting was not introduced to the Printing Office until 1950. On the brick wall above the shop front was the HERALD OFFICE in large letters. In 1967 Mr. J. Hall took over the business, he launched the Midweek Herald in 1982. In 1987 he retired and the business became C M L, (Community Media Ltd.). The papers no longer printed in the town. The printing machine is now in the Sidmouth Museum. The shop name changed to LEWIS MEESON by 1991. Next as MARTIN, Newsagent.

Crossing over East Street. (formerly known as Theatre Lane.)

Devonshire House.

15.   This was a thatched house. The front door with a window on the left side, and a bay window on the right. In 1856 two cottages were for sale and were bought by W. Tuck and R. Price. These may have been behind the house.

Around 1830, Elizabeth Avery, Shopkeeper, dealer in Sundries and Mr. George Avery, Cooper. By 1850, Mr. George Avery, Grocery and Wine, House Agents. Mr. James Avery, Woollen Draper 1857, also a receiver for the Devon and Exeter Savings Bank. Mr. G. Avery died in 1886, the business was purchased by Mr. Phillip Sadler, who ran the shop and bar for seven months and went bankrupt in 1887. Also we have the name of Edward Bowden, who took over in November 1877 to October 1879. In January Mrs. Bearn, Fancy Goods. Then John Casson. At the back of the shop a sitting room or parlour was made into a Drinking Bar, with an entrance from East Street and called the SADDLERS ARMS in 1886. In the September of 1886, the dwelling house, including shop, bar, parlour, kitchen, cellars and two store rooms, were on lease to Mr. Lethbridge. They were sold to Mr Saddler for £775. The two adjoining Cottages in Theatre Lane were also sold. Mr. W. Pinney, Music Teacher stayed at Mr Avery's in 1868, he left Sidmouth in 1870.

By 1850 (Harvey's directory) there was a post Office in Fore Street, Mr. Reuben Barratt, Postmaster. In 1887 the Post Office moved to here from the Market Place. Mrs. Lucy Rainger, Postmistress followed by Mrs. Georgina Barratt. The Post Office was open weekdays 7.00 am to 8.00 pm and Sunday 7.00 to 10.00 am. Letters posted before 2.00 pm delivered the same afternoon. There was a large Post Office clock hanging over the pavement. The last postmaster was Mr. T. Long. The Post Office closed in February 1938. It then became Number 15. SANDERS Estate Agent and Auction rooms until 1952. TIMOTHY WHITE Chemist, 1953. MAYFIELDS, Drapers in 1968, changing to a Grocers, HOBSONS Market to 1979. The shop was empty for a short time to about 1980 when AXE Supermarket opened. Then as SPAR in December 1990 to February 1992, opened later in the year as LENTON of Sidmouth, Ladies and Menswear, until they moved to the High Street.

In 1995 the shop was empty for several months. In March 1996 opened as DELDERFIELDS. Antiques. Mr Richard Eley.

Mates Guide

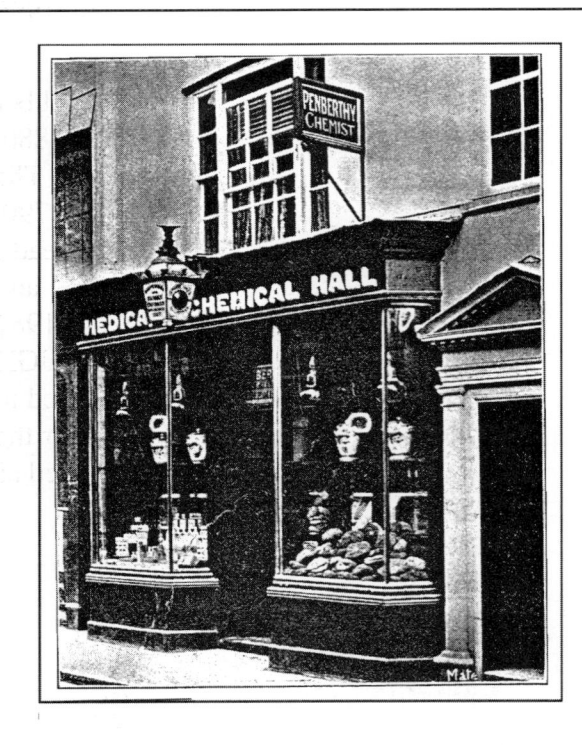

H. B. Penberthy,
Chemist (Member of the Pharmaceutical Society).
Established 1817.

Physicians' Prescriptions accurately dispensed at all hours, day or night, by fully qualified dispensers only.
Surgical Appliances and Chemical Apparatus. Homœopathic Medicines.
—— Water Beds on Sale or Hire. ——
India-rubber Bottles, Cushions, Pillows, &c.
Photographic Chemicals. Dark Room.
—— Mineral Waters of all kinds. ——
Aerated Water in Syphon and Bottle.

Veterinary Chemist.

—— All Cases treated in absence of ——
Mr. T. S. NEWBURY, M.R.C.V.S. (LOND.), F.R.V M.S., ETC., who visits Sidmouth every Thursday, or by special request. Orders —— taken by H. B. PENBERTHY. ——
Horse and Cattle Medicines

Note the Address:
Chemical and Medical Hall,
Next the Post Office, **Sidmouth.**

Fore Street

14.   The first date and trade for here is for a Chemist Shop, Chemical and Medical Hall in 1817. The first name is Mr. Atkins in 1824. Mr. Edwards for 1850. To Rowland Chessall, Pharmaceutical Chemist 1862, also Dentist and Stamp Office, still here in 1897. Henry Broad Penberthy in the Market Place in 1883 moving to here by 1901. HOLMAN and HAM and Co.Ltd.1914 Chemist. In 1970, CHANDLERS, boating accessories, closing in March 1999, Nancy Barons then moved here from the opposite side of Fore Street, with their fruit and vegetable business, calling it BARONS of Sidmouth. Closed in October 1999. In September 2000 the shop opened as Call SAVE, Mobile 'Phones.

Middle House.
    A house with the front door on the left, with a pillar on each side with gable porch roof. This was later to be changed to a shop front with the door in the middle. Susan Pullin, Chemist with her son Thomas in 1851. Mr James Loveridge Draper, moved to here from

Temple Street by 1910, the last date for him trading here is 1923. The next reference is for OLIVES, Gowns and Dresses, Mrs. Gatrell-Smith, in 1926. Mrs. R. Stickland, in 1935 and the last name Mrs. D. Martin, in June 1962 to March 1984. In the May, Simon Pollentine opened as SIDMOUTH CARD CENTRE. Town and Country Prints in 1988. In 1990 changed to WOOLLIES, Woollens and Knitwear.

12. John Benjamin Webber and Sons, Bakers, were here in 1851, by 1857 John Webber also Biscuit maker in 1870. was taken over by William Owen Shepherd and Son in 1880, Baker, Confectioner, Coffee and Refreshment Rooms. Mr. Shepherd died in July 1885. The property was put up for sale by his family, but did not reach the reserve, withdrawn at £790. The next name is George Harris Russell in 1891, Luncheon Rooms. Also sold 'Fancy Bread', Cadburys Chocolates and advertised 'Comfortable Accommodation for Tourists and Commercial Gentlemen'. It became a shoe shop by 1925, STEAD and SIMPSON until 1982 when the shop was up for sale. Then in June 1982 a different trade, GAINSBOROUGH HOUSE Antiques, Kim Scratchley. In 1985 a new shop front was put in. The shop closed in April 1995, when he moved to new shop units in Libra Court. There was a short let for the Christmas period in 1995 as TREATS, Sweets etc. Then empty for a time. In 1996 opened as LOOK, Perfumes and Accessories. In July 1998, SIDMOUTH OUTDOOR Co.

J. Ankins

Fore Street, 1973

October 16th, 1899

Bovett House.
11.   A thatched house made into two shops. The first reference as a shop is 1833. H Bovett, Boot and Shoe Dealer. By 1889 James Bovett. In 1899 it was closed for alterations and became Samuel Henry Mortimore, Boot and Shoe Makers, a reference date of 1910. The name changes in 1919 to Charles Mortimore. News agents and Bill Poster. The next date and trade which we have for here is for FREETH'S TOFFEES Ltd., who were here in 1926. Next was THE SPINNING WHEEL, a Wool shop in the mid 1940s, when they moved from New Street and were here until 1973. Next BOOTS, Chemist had both shops (Numbers 11 and 10) converted into one large shop with all new shop fronts.

Sidmouth Directory and Advertiser

CUMMINGS' SHAMPOOING SALOON,
OPPOSITE THE LONDON HOTEL,

Hair brushed by the Rotary Brush.

Fancy Toy Warehouse.

FORE STREET, SIDMOUTH.

1868

10. We have a reference for Mr. S. Turner, Men's Hairdresser from New Street, in September 1851 and James Turner in New Street, 1856. Cummings', Shampooing Saloon and Fancy Toy Warehouse, 1868-1883. We also have the name F. H. Baker, Ladies' and Gentleman's Hairdresser, advertised in 1894 as opposite Royal London Hotel, so must have been here. In the early 1902, Tommy Haselock, here until 1920. Next it became, Arthur IRISH, Hairdresser and Tobacconist. The Tobacco was sold in the front of the shop and the gentleman went through the shop to a room at the back to have their hair cut. In 1929, Mr. Arthur Irish, Mr. Elliot Breach and Garage owner, Mr. Hodge, had Sidmouth's first Motor Ambulance, St. John Ambulance. 'Sympathy' a model 'A' Ford. Mr. Irish was in the Forces in the war and came back to the shop in January 1945 (the shop name did not change). closing in 1973. The next change was to BOOTS, Chemists.

W. Wagstaff

The Restored "Sympathy" taken in 1998

77

Osborne House.

9. In the 1856 directory it lists Mr. John Potbury, Ironmonger and Coal Merchant. Fore Street. this must have been his private house, not his work place. He was still here in 1878. We also have the name, Mrs. Sellek's School, 'English Education with accommodation if desired', for a new term starting in 1875. In 1874 a Mr. Harding, Professor of music.

This is the only place where we can fit in the next three shops, which are in the 1851 census, Pitwood, Burgin, Cridland, at numbers 9, 7, 5, Mr. William Pitwood, Coal and Slate dealer to 1866, Mrs. Charlotte Pitwood, Draper and Milliner, 1851, Pitwood and Force, Milliners and Dressmakers, in 1869-1870. The next reference for here is as 'Havana House'. Daniel Lightfoot Robertson, Tobacconist and Fancy goods, 1893-1897. He was trading in New Street in 1883-1892. Mr. J. POWER in 1903, Tobacconist into the 1920s. By 1934, Mr. W. N. Trump. and Frank Weston in the 1960s. Still called Havana House. It then became MAYNARDS, Confectioners until October 1984. JILL'S Confectioners to 1986 and then called JARS. Next Mr. A. Dergin Cards shop, closing in 1991. July 1993 a new Trade, Tea and Coffee Rooms and Restaurant, OSBORNES. Mr. and Mrs. G. Troman.

J. Ankins

Bottom Fore Street, 1973

7.   Miss Martha Burgin, Berlin Wool Depository about 1850 to 1890. John LAKE and Sons Omnibus Office 1890 to 1906, agents for London and South Western Railway Co. In 1910 J. Lake and Son, Jobmasters. The next trade here may have been, Mr. V. G. Smith, Men's Outfitters in 1931. Changed to Radio and Electrical business, Norman HUCK, opened in1946 to 1983. Mr. Huck's father was manager for Gilbert Gilkes and Gordon Ltd., Electrical Contractors who carried out a lot of early work in Sidmouth, and they were in Foundry Yard. In May 1983 change to NOTIONS, Fabric, Haberdashery. May 1991 Hairdressers, CHANGES. Tricia Fewell. In 1996 Fiona Rose.

5.   Mr. John Cridland, Grocer, China and Glass, early 1850s-1860s. cannot find any more names until in 1893, Thomas Underdown, Florist and Fruiterer. Next became EASTMANS, Butchers, in 1902-1906. Changed to FRISBY, Footwear, 1918. After closing in 1983, the shop was empty for a long time, then opening as a shoe shop, TANDEM to March 1988. Next SUE RYDER, charity shop and in June 1992 another Charity shop, MARIE CURIE, Cancer Care.

The next building stands out from the others, with part of the side of the building facing up Fore Street. Around 1854 the building, known as the SIDMOUTH INSTITUTION, was used as a reading room. On Monday 16th. February 1880, a large and influential meeting was held at the vicarage to consider whether a Coffee Tavern could be established in the town. After several meetings it was decided to rent this building. A Joint Stock Company was formed later in 1880 to spend £30 for repairs to outside of the building. Alterations were made to the interior, the front room fitted with a counter and requirements of a refreshment room. The old cottage adjoining it at the back, was made into one large room, and a new floor and large window added. The room at the back was made into a kitchen and scullery. There was a large room upstairs for reading and writing. The cost of alterations and furniture amounting to about £120. It opened as the COFFEE TAVERN in January 1881, 6am to 10pm. Mr. George Macke, as Manager. The names of Withers and Blackmore, refreshment rooms. Reading Room the OLD COFFEE TAVERN to Mr. and Mrs. William (Bill) Skinner, 1892. Robert George HUCKER, refreshment rooms by 1919. Earnest Hucker, 1926.

Mrs. Hucker, Café and Commercial Hotel in 1935. Next name change to MAGNOLIA Café in August 1950. Then back to old name, The OLD COFFEE TAVERN. Next as THE RESTAURANT in the 1960s, bought by Mr. Sambati in 1968. This closed in the early 1970s and reopened as KNIGHTS as part of their shop next door. This part of the main shop is now called VANITY FAYRE, as part of KNIGHTS.

Spohr House.
    Mr. W. Pinney, Professor of Music, may have been in the flat over the shop in 1868. Mr. H. P. SAWDAY, Pianos, Musical Instruments, in the mid 1800s. In 1886 Smiths Music Saloon opened. By 1889 H. Bartlett Music Salon to 1902.

LONDON HOUSE, SIDMOUTH

One of the Oldest Drapery Establishments in the County of Devon

W. H. BUNCE

Holds a large Stock of Household and Family Linen, Cotton Sheetings, Calicoes, Flannels, Blankets, &c., of the Best Makes, at the lowest paying prices.
Fashionable Dress Materials, Mantles, Millinery, Lace, Hosiery, Gloves, &c.

DRESS AND MANTLE MAKING

Under experienced and skilful management—good fit, style and work guaranteed, at most moderate charges.

Japanese, Chinese, Indian, German, Swiss, French and British Articles of use and ornament suitable for presents, from One Penny to 80 Guineas.

2½ % Discount for prompt Cash.

From a Photo by J. A. Bellinger, Sidmouth

SPOHR HOUSE, SIDMOUTH

H. P. SAWDAY

Pianos by the best Makers at lowest co-operative prices for Cash
Estey American Organs and Harmoniums, Violins, Guitars, Banjos, Flutes, Fifes, Flageolets, Melodeons, Concertinas, Musical Boxes, and every variety of small Musical Instruments

Pianos on Hire, and on the 3 years system. Tuning and Repairs

All new music as soon as published.

Spohr House is a branch of H. P. Sawday's, George Street, Plymouth, one of the largest Music Establishments in England.

Avertisement dated 1870

Next it became TREBY EARL, Miss Dean, Ladies Outfitters to 30th. July 1960 when they closed and KNIGHTS took over with their shop next door.

London House.

In 1850 George SAWDAY, Linen and Woollen, Drapers, employing five shop assistants, also agents to the Star Life and Manchester Fire Office, to June 1870 when it became W. H. BUNCE, Drapery. In 1884 Mr. Bunce built an extension to the premises and opened a Music Salon. In February 1886 it changed to H. Tuckwell. Closed for a short time in September 1892, and opened as BON MARCHÉ. In 1901 BELLE VUE RESTAURANT and Temperance Hotel, Mr. W. Hellman Proprietor.

In 1913 a complete change to become, ELLIS LITTLE CINEMA. A short piece in the Sidmouth Observer of February 1913 describes, 'a roomy entrance hall, painted an inviting shade of crimson, floor in a terra-cotta colour, a pretty pay box on either side double swing doors leading to the seats. Inside here the front is formed of two arches richly ornamented with plaster decorations and at night outlined with rows of electric lamps'. In 1919 THE CINEMA PICTURE PALACE. The cinema closed in 1936. For a short time it was used as Crazy Golf. Empty until 1937 when it was bought by Mr. G. W. KNIGHT. Ladies Outfitters, still KNIGHTS today.

Cliff Rescue Team, Selley's Yard

Back Row: *Rob Johns, Pete Daniels, Ray Oldrey, Ron Jenkins, Ken Connant, Roy Daniels, Malcombe Gorman, Roy Gorman, Les Westcott, Charlie Snow*

Seated Front Row: *Ken Chick, George Gooding, Fred Quaintance*

Through the archway was the London Yard, Stables and yard for the ROYAL LONDON HOTEL. The yard and Stables also had an entrance from Russell Street, extending at the back of the shops. The horse drawn coaches started from here for Exeter, Taunton and Honiton. Two of the coaches were called, Defiance and Telegraph.

About 1912, called Selley's Yard, this then comprised various small units and trades over the years. A Slaughter House for the Butchers on the corner with Fore Street. The First Church of Christ Scientist. Sid Vale Mineral Works until about 1914. Mr. W. Snow, Plumber in the mid 1940s. Charles Solman, Mineral water maker here in 1919-1935. Sidmouth Ice works here in 1935-1947. Mr. G. B. Carter started here with a workshop, later to move into the High Street. Hills Garage, 1980s. Barrett & Gigg, Cabinet Makers, workshop.

St. John Ambulance 1949-1960. South West Typewriting Service, Alan and Pat Tully, in the mid 1960s. They produced a local paper called the Sidmouth News, this proved unsuccessful and only ran for a short time in the 1970s. Westcountry Woodland Products 1969. In July 1992 part of the south side was altered and changed to new small units, called LIBRA COURT, a Craft Centre with an additional entrance from York Street.

Frith Post Card

Lower Fore Street

Libra House.
    Part of this house is over the archway to Selley's yard. In the 1960s a large double sided clock hung on the wall over the archway above the pavement.
Libra House Flat over the archway and shop. This was an office for Turouands Babton Mayiew and Co. Ware Ward and Co. In the early 1950s. Office Turouand Youngs and Co. Chartered Accountants in 1966. Character Cottages in the mid 1970s. then a change to ALAN ROWE Gents Hairdressing in September 1983. With Tricia Fewell in August 1989, until she moved to her own shop in August 1991. Mr. A. Rowe closed in 1999.

    We are now back onto Fore Street, and the last shops on this side of the road. The building as far as York Street was probably a house and two cottages before being made into three shops. We have references for 1851, William Arundall, Coach man. Mrs. Rebecca Voysey and John Searle, family dress Makers and Milliners.
By the archway the first dates as a shop was W. F. SELLEK, Butcher, in the mid 1860 to1879.

We then have the names, all Butchers, Alfred Hellier, about 1897. Mr. H. Bolt then ran the business for a time. After Mr. Bolt, there was a Mr. Ernest Burgoin in 1900. About 1912 SELLEY Brothers, still Butchers. It had a new shop front with the door moved to the left side of the shop. In 1952 the trade changed to Estate Agents, to the mid 1960s. T. SANDERS and STAFF. Then Thomas Sanders and Andrew Redfern and Co. Again a new shop window. LESTER SMITH in 1966 to March 1984. To ANDREW CHARLES, then The PRUDENTIAL in 1989 to 1990. All estate agents. After the Pru. closed it was empty for a while until a short let as a Souvenir and gift shop 1991. CARLESS and BARTHOLOMEW, Oculist and Optician, opened in November 1994. In mid 2001 name changed to BENNETT & ROGERS, still an opticians.

Next there were two shops.

The first shop here was BELLINGERS, Photographer, Picture frame maker in 1884-1902. An advert in 1892 states 'shop near the Esplanade'. we also have a reference for Buchanan-Wollaston and Co. photographic material dealers, 'The Western Studio' for 1897-1902. In 1906 G. T. Harris, Photographer, he produced a number of Sidmouth post cards, here to about 1911.

The Summerland by The Sea

1922

The other shop in 1893, John Lake, Posting, Livery stables and Mail Contractor. Next Alfred Deans Booking Office, Droshky and Carriages in late 1890s. A Droshky was a small four wheeled carriage, used as a taxi. Next 'Punky' Downs Booking Office.

In 1905, the two shops were amalgamated into one shop, THOMAS H. RODD. Gentleman's Outfitter. This was a large shop with a hardwood Floor and a long wooded top counter. The cash desk was at the back of the shop, Miss Gooding ran the pay desk for many years. There was a large fitting room with seats, and a very fine oak staircase led up to the first floor.

In July 1986 the shop was divided into two shops again, the left side stayed as Rodds until September 1999 when they moved to the Market Place. In April 2000, IVOR CORAM. Footwear Specialist.

The new shop became CHILDS and Co. Building Society Consultants, until 1993. Change of trade to the HANDMADE LACE COMPANY, until April 1998 when they moved into Old Fore Street. Next a new trade. THE ANIMAL ZONE, Pet Shop to October 1999. Empty until July 2001 when W. H. Smith opened for a three month short let. Now empty.

On the other side of the turning to York Street. The York Pub part of the York Hotel. A meeting room. First meeting of the Corinthian Club (Sailing Club) 28th. July 1894 was held here. Later to be Antique shops. Sampson Wade in 1919-1926. Miss Beatrice F. Fagan was here in the 1930 to 1948. Then became Harold Allen, H. Scratchley and H. Locke, Antiques. Changed to Joy Chambers in 1978 to March 1982.

Then became the York Tapp Bar, by 1998 TAPPERS, as part of the York Hotel.

We can now go back up Fore Street to the West side, starting at the end of The High Street.

FORE STREET, WEST SIDE

Veal and Coulson Stores

    The shop on the corner is a three storey building part of which faces up the High Street. Originally it had large sash windows on the second and third floors, many of them were later taken out and bricked up. The front of the shop faces onto Fore Street. This side of the shop had the door on the left, with two very large plate glass windows on the right, to the end of the building, and two windows on the High Street side. The first reference, for HENRY DAWE, Family Grocer, (est.1809) here to 1874. We also have the name W. G. HARRIS about 1822-1866. Next it became, COULSON BROTHERS in 1876, Family Grocers and Provision Merchants, they had a very large sign over the shop, ANGLO-BAVARIAN ALES and STOUT. They unfortunately became bankrupt in 1900.

    Mr. T. B. Veale bought the premises. In 1901 it was also a House Agents. The name, VEALE'S of SIDMOUTH, was painted in large letters, high up on the wall looking up the High Street.

Sidmouth Museum

Veal's Corner

Mr. Veale, specialised in mature Cheddar Cheese. He bought up to twenty huge cheeses and stored them in the upper store where they had to be turned at regular intervals until ready for sale[19]. He also had a rare privilege, he bottled his own Guinness. A great cask would arrive from Dublin and put in the cellar, then two men would spend days bottling and labeling them, Harp Guinness. The shop traded under the name Veale's into the 1960s. When it changed to HOME AND COLONIAL, Grocers. New shop fronts were put in and a new doorway made in the end window looking up the High Street. Then it became, LIPTONS, Grocers. They were here in 1976, to the end of the 1970s. The trade changed to a Gift shop by 1980, SIDMOUTH GIFT CENTRE. Later TOCATI and TRAVEL STYLE, now called TRAVEL STYLE.

Next to the shop, there was a proportioned doorway to the house, the building was built in face brick work, later all plastered and painted. Next to the door there were notice and poster advertisement boards. Became Veale's Bar in 1824. About 1900, VEALE SPIRIT STORES. Later the GRAPES INN. This became popular as a tradesman's pub.

Sidmouth Museum

Home and Colonial, Fore Street

They were granted a full 'Off' licence in August 1962. This was all to change when LIPTONS, put in new shop front and made the ground floor into part of their shop. JOHN BRUNT, opened a WINE SHOP, later to become T. FOSTER, about 1965, to about 1978 when there was a complete change of trade to BRIGGS, Shoe shop. By 1999 the shop was bought by Stead and Simpsons, but keeping the name Briggs.

2.	The next shop down the road, first name and date which we have come across is, William Perryman, Master Boot maker in 1851. In 1890, H. F. Sellek, known as 'Long Harry', an advert in a guide book states, 'Established 1865'. Then Harry 'Parson' Sellek, (Congregational Church). Painter and Decorator, employing a small team of painters. The shop sold artists sundries, around 1907 to the mid 1920s. Mr. and Mrs. Bessie Davies,

Mates Guides

Harry F. Sellek
Established 1865
Member National Association of Master House Painters & Decorators.

House Decorator.
Glazier &
Paperhangings Merchant.
Dealer in Artists' Colours and Materials.

Fore St Sidmouth.

1907

THE BINOCULAR SHOP, Watchmakers and Jewellers to 1984. It became a CAFE-RESTAURANT, Mr. E. Crisp and D. Harris. Then to a Ladies Outfitters, ELAINE MURRAY in 1986, and for sale in 1991. Reopening as CHOICES in 1994.

3. The only early date we can find for this site is John Potbury, Ironmongers and Coal Merchant. In the 1930s, it was part of Russell's china shop next door. By 1937 we believe it had become a Dress Shop, an advert for 'Brounette, Gowns' was advertised in 1937. Later to PAWLINS, Ladies Outfitters, in the 1940s. The next reference which we have is for P. Yendell and Co. in 1968. In 1959 Mr. Dennis Bennett, Manager, in 1968 he bought the business. Called YENDELLS, Men's Outfitters.

4. A shop and warehouse, Mr. Thomas Sellek, China and Glass dealer, here in 1870. Mrs. Ellen Sellek, in 1902. By 1906 changed to Mr. Reggie RUSSELL'S, Glass and China Store about 1914, this was a large shop on two floors, to September 1968. In the 1970s, PETER DOMINIC, Wine Shop. In 1992, changed of name, to THRESHERS, same trade.

The NEW INN early 1800s. Also an Inland Revenue office in 1852. EBDON'S COMMERCIAL HOTEL, by 1906. Duffett's COMMERCIAL in the 1930. THE BLACK HORSE INN in the1960s.

40. Thomas F. Stone, Carver and Guilder, lived here in 1851-1870. Also John Stone Carpenter and Shopkeeper 1857-1870. It was altered into car showrooms in the 1890s, for Sidmouth Motor Co. It must have had a large opening or sliding doors as there was room for two cars on show and a office. The company was started by Mr. Reg Griffin and Mr. Bert Lewis, later Mr. Dagworthy, Sidmouth Motor Co. Later to move to the Western Garage on the sea front. At one time he had three motor coaches with the names, Forgetmenot, Poppy and Carnation. One of his descendants, Tom Griffiths, has the deckchair concession on the Esplanade and his sister and brother-in-law, Wendy and Roger Markham until recently ran the Kiosk on the Bedford Lawn Car Park.

Next as a Toy Shop, H. Lake 1920s. Mr Harold Turner, Clock and Watchmaker, 1937. Next Mr. Hawkins, Men's Tailors. Change of trade to RADIANT Dry Cleaners in August 1938. VANITY FAIR, Ladies Dress and Gowns. Next The BURNLEY Building Society. Changed to the NATIONAL PROVINCIAL, 1983. This closed as it became part of The ABBEY NATIONAL PLC. Shop empty for a time, then opened as a Picture shop called ROCK POOL FINE ART.

31. The only early reference which we can find for the next building is that a Mr. William Beaves lived here in 1851, a master Bootmaker. Next the name Skinner, Honiton Lace 1914 to late 1920s. And afterwards to a Toy shop. It then became JOHNSONS, Dyers and Cleaners in 1930 to 1952. BOLLOMS were next and continued the same trade into the 1970s, The name BOLLOMS is still in mosaic tiles in the doorway

(2001). Change of trade to RAYGLOW, Discount shoes in July 1981. FEET FIRST, Shoes to December 1982. Mr. Marc Winstanley, GET FRESH, Fruit and Veg. In May 1988 changed to Sidmouth DELICATESSEN, closing in August 1991. Next, it became THE MOUSE TRAP to 1994. Then COUNTRY BLOOMERS, 1995, Dried flower decorations.

Next door may have been called, Devon House. In 1851 this was the home of Thomas Callalott, Saddler, employing a boy. Then in 1897, William H. LAKE, Corn Dealer and Saddler, by 1902, Corn Dealer and Seedsman. Bill Lake, supplied most of the farmers for miles around, the poultry keepers and bird fanciers with bird seed. Around the shop were wooden bins, a big scoop measured out what was required and weighed. About 1940 it became, W. FRENCH and Co., Corn and Seed Merchants. Then a change of trade to GRANTS, Wine Bar and then SHERIDANS, in the 1980s. The shop closed for a few months in 1986, and Mr. John Doddrell, opened, keeping the same trade name. In 1991 BROWNS, Wine Bar and Bistro, Richard and Katherine Brown. In 1999 Andrew and Jenny Roy.

34.   Susanna F. Hoyte, Book Seller and Stationer, with a staff of one man and a boy in 1850, also on two Wednesdays a month, The Messrs Mosely, Surgeon Dentists in attendance from their Exeter shop, here into the 1880s. Next JOHN FIELD, Tailor, Outfitter and Hatter, late 1880s. Name changed to J. FIELD and SON, Then changed to just FIELDS, keeping to a Men's Outfitters shop to April 1978. Next a complete change when CHARACTER COTTAGES moved from Libra House. This was a Self Catering Holidays business, manager Bill Shapland. It was taken over in 1978 by BEACH VILLA TRAVEL, suddenly closing on February 25th. 1993. Shop empty until 1994, when it opened as SUE RYDER, Charity shop to 1996. On May 17th opened as The BRITISH HEART FOUNDATION, another charity shop.

In 1851 William Berry, Boot maker. Nicholas J. Uglow, Jeweller, Watchmaker, 1866 to mid 1920s. BOOTS Chemists in the 1930s to 1980. Then to a Building Society, ABBEY NATIONAL. Now a bank ABBEY NATIONAL PLC.

We now come to CROSS LANE. (Trumps Lane). A narrow lane between the shops. On the South side is Cosmopolitan House, this was Trumps Off Licence. Then to WHOLE FOODS in 1984. REGENCY CLEANERS opening in January 1985. C M C INSURANCE and INVESTMENT April 1986. Antique shop in 1995.

On the North side. JEN STYLE opened in March 1982 Ladies' and Gentlemen's Hair Fashions to 1992. THE VILLAGE COBBLER opened in October 1994, with KEY SECURITY as well later. Then to a gift and china shop and in 1997, The FEEL GOOD FACTORY, closed in July 1999. In 2001, as MAD GOBLIN MINIATURES.

Back into Fore Street.

This corner used to be two cottages, Spencer and Churchill. In 1813 Cosmopolitan

House was built on the site. Richard STONE and GOVE Grocers. In 1836, there was a Miss Sarah Grove, William Grove and Mr. John Trump Grocer, Wine merchant, House agent and agent for the Imperial Fire and Life Office in 1850. In 1870s it was TRUMP BROS. John and William. In November 1877 the partnership ended. In 1897 it was advertised as THE COSMOPOLITAN STORES. Next as TRUMPS, William Trump, Grocers, Bakers, Wine Merchants. They roasted the coffee beans and bottled their wine at the back of the shop on the Old Fore Street side. Most of the goods were bought in bulk and weighed out and packed by hand in their own Trumps Stores wrappers. Trumps Stores had branches in Axminster by 1910, Colyton and Ottery St. Mary by 1919, Seaton and Beer by 1926. Their advertising and on all their vans said 'DEVON'S BEST'. Their garages and yard were in East Street. The shop had a overhead wire 'railway' set up, each counter had a wire to the cash desk at the back of the shop with a container to take the bill and money, a spring loaded handle sent it along the wire for the cashier to stamp 'paid' and the change given, and then sent back to the counter. Each counter had a chair for customers. The shop stayed in the Trump family until 1971 when it was sold. The shop has had different owners, but still has the name TRUMP over the shop door and inlayed in the tiled step at the entrance.

The next shop, There was a James Colwill, market gardener in All Saints Road in 1883. We do not have dates for Colwill, Florists and Greengrocer, who we think was here before, Charles Alfred BERWICK, Fruiterers 1894-1919. No more references until 1930 when it had become HOME and COLONIAL Stores, Grocers to mid 1960s. KAN TONG, Chinese Restaurant opened in August 1966. April 1971, HOMES and KITCHEN. Next change of name to PAPER MOON, Bernard Tomkin. In September 1999, Mr. and Mrs. Tony Garland.

Mr. C. Farrant, Ironmongers, also a reference as a Draper and Milliners, in 1822 to 1850. Walter Prettejohn, Ironmonger and Tin Plate worker, 1852. J. H. Hews before C. A. MAEER, Peak Farm Dairy, Butchers, Poultry 1877. Next it may have been Langbridge, Flowers about 1918-1926. Septimus BARRATT Book shop to mid 1930s. Edward ROWE, Stationers in 1935 and then W. H. SMITH, followed by P. R. and M. RATHBONE in 1973 to April 1986, both Stationers and Bookshops. Change to NEW LOOK, clothes shop open August 1986.

The LONDON INN is the corner site with New Street. One of the oldest Inns in Sidmouth. Later called The LONDON HOTEL. In the early 1800s, on the ground floor were The Assembly Rooms, which could hold up to 200 people. Balls and dances were held here. There were also Billiard and Card rooms. In 1866 they had 'Penny Readings', a programme which lasted about two hours, the entrance and programme charge was a Penny. Short stories were read, there were duets and comic songs and the National Anthem. Touring companies put on various attractions. In 1869, one of these was The Original Buckleys Continental Star Troupe of Minstrels, gave a grand concert. In the 1870s Drama Groups, some shows ran for six days, and Choral Society shows. Various entertainment was put on by local people. Around 1878 the Inn had stables and a slaughter house on the other side of the street, in the London Yard. (Selley's Yard). The Hotel premises were partly rebuilt in 1986 making two new shops on the ground floor on the Fore Street side and one on the corner with New Street.

The three new Shops were.

CARDS and THINGS open 1987. In August 1999, Tea Rooms opened on the first floor, in part of the London Hotel, entrance in the back of the shop. On 15th May 2000 it changed to the London Tea Rooms. Still Cards and Things, shop on the ground floor.

NANCY BARON, Greengrocers 1987, in April 1999 they moved to the other side of the road into No.14 formerly the Chandlers shop. In May 1999 opened as The Edinburgh Woollen Mill.

FREEMAN HARDY WILLIS, Shoe shop on the corner. Which changed to STEAD and SIMPSON in 1989.

Cross over NEW STREET to the shops up to Dove Lane.

The corner shop was Richard Stone, Hostler, with a poultry shop run by his wife Mary in 1850. Richard Stone Greengrocer in 1857-1870. DEVON and BRISTOL SUPPLY STORES, in the 1890s. W. C. Symes was proprietor in 1892. SYMES and Co., Grocers, in 1893, by December they had moved to New Street, in part of the newly altered London Hotel. The next date and name which we have is, 1923, The STAR SUPPLY STORES and STAR TEA Co. Next change was to INTERNATIONAL STORES in 1936. Then alterations for THE MIDLAND BANK, which opened in 1959, in 1999 renamed HSBC.

There are two shops before Dove Lane. One of these may have been Mr. John Pile, Ironmonger in 1824. The first of the two shops. Mr. Charles Snell, Tailor, in 1851. In 1889, Theophilus Mortimore, Poulterer and Game dealer, by 1893, he was a Bill Poster and Town Crier. In 1910, he was also a Newsagent. 1926 Charles Mortimore, Bill Poster and Town Crier to the mid 1930s. Then changed to RUSSELLS, China to August 1966. Mr. White, BETTING SHOP in the 1970s. ALLANS Wool shop 1980s. In April 1989, K. M. J. ELECTRICAL to June 1991. Then in July, THE UPPER CRUST BAKERY.

The house next to Dove Lane was occupied by Mr. Thomas Heard, Coach Painter, his wife Sarah a Dressmaker 1850s. Then as a shop 'Gent' Yeo's, Boot and Shoe repairs, here in 1910, after trading in Ham Cottages, Sid Road around 1906. by 1926 he had moved to Eaton Terrace in Temple Street. In 1919 Mrs. Amella O'Brien had a Newsagents shop into the late 1920s. we believe it was here until she moved to Prospect Place. Mr. Alfred Dean to Douglas Dean in 1935, Taxi Booking Office, Post cards, Tobacconist, Confectioner. The shop was managed by Miss Daisy Dean (Sister), whilst Douglas ran the Garage and Taxi business situated on the Esplanade. When Miss Dean died. Mrs. Pearl Dean (Wife of Derek) took over the running of the shop, which was called DEANS to February 1983. She sold Toys as well as Tobacco and Confectionery. Next FRIENDLY REST Bed linen to 1986. To GANESHA WHOLEFOOD, Penny and Fred Easton in June 1986, moving to The Shopping Centre in May 1996. Now ladies hairdressers, JANE TODD, who is a granddaughter of the late Douglas Dean, August 1996.

Turning for Dove Lane.

The Dove Inn, an old Sidmouth Pub from at least the mid 1800s. For sale in 1898, sold to a Mr. Martin. Later from about 1914 it was run for many years by the Prideaux family. In July 1997 when it was changed to FINNS. In January 2001, Gary and Tracey Williams took over and refurbished the building and opened under the old name THE DOVE closed in November 2001.

The last building before Kings Lane, was HIGH HALL, built by Mr Denby in mid 1800s. Also have the name, Carslade 1841-1857, Lodgings and shoe repair. The house was made into a Café and opened on August 30th 1901, as TRUMPS CAFÉ, Edwin Grove Trump, Cake and Sweet shop on the ground floor, The Café Restaurant was on the second and third floors. In 1931 it changed owners, FORTE'S (Devon) Ltd. Restaurant and Café. In 1937 the Café de Luxe, G. Forte. In the 1960s The HOUSE OF TEDBURY. Next it became THE TAVERN. then LEGENDS and now THE NEW TAVERN.

At the back of the building it has an entrance onto Dove Lane. This was TRUMPS WINTER GARDENS, a large room with polished maple wood floor and large lantern shaped glass roof, used for dances, parties, exhibitions, music evenings. One of these was the Ted James Band, who used to play for afternoon tea in the early 1920s. A Mr. Twitchett, played the piano in the summer, 4 p.m. to 6 p.m. Another group was the Catherine Startup Ladies Orchestra, also about 1920.

Mr. Fred Tedbury had one of the first 'Pye, Black box' record players, one could go in and have a tea or coffee and listen to classical music. He was very keen on Gilbert and Sullivan and often had Gilbert and Sullivan afternoons or evenings. The Winter Gardens now sadly changed to low ceiling and dark Disco Bar, Night Club. DIMENTIONS in 1988. And now CARINAS.

Over Kings Lane to the last shops before the sea front, this was the DOMESTIC BAZAAR, around 1914. Then the Penny Bazaar, which sold nothing over 6d. ($2\frac{1}{2}$p). Cheap souvenirs etc. Next the MOCHA Café, Confectionery, Cake shop about 1918. In the 1930s, THE GIFT SHOP, Mr. Frank Stokes, later Mr. J. Govier, THE GIFT SHOP. In the 1980s called ALL THINGS BRIGHT and BEAUTIFUL. In June 1999, new owners, Laura and Martin Drew.

Temple House was the residence of Miss Maguire. About 1872 it was on lease to the LONDON and SOUTH WESTERN BANK. For Sale by auction at the York Hotel on May 30th 1881, but did not reach the reserve of £1500. Having started on May 14th 1863 in Hope Cottage, Mr. Radford and his partner, Mr. Williams, had extensive alterations made before moving to here. Later to merge with the LONDON and PROVINCIAL Bank in 1917. In 1918 became BARCLAYS. They then moved to the High Street in 1932. It became the DEVON and EXETER SAVINGS BANK. In the 1970s it was sold and GOVIER made it into his GIFT SHOP. Sadly all the imposing stone work, windows and door were taken out and a plain shop front put in.

Frith Postcard

Looking up Fore Street from Esplanade

NEW STREET

We have been unable to accurately place each name to an individual shop, those listed in the directories as being in New Street. The Trades and Names are; Mr. Turner, Hairdresser in 1856 - 1886. Mr. James Gibbs, Jeweller, who had a shop in the High Street in 1856, by 1878 he had moved to New Street. Mr. J. S. Endacott, Greengrocer in 1930, until he moved to Mill Street by 1939.

There was a great fire on 27th January, 1902. Five shops burnt down. A newspaper report stated that the fire was stopped before destroying the London Hotel and Belle Vue Dairy. Shops destroyed in the fire: Lakes, Booking Office, Mr. E. Casson, Grocer, Mr. G. T. Evans, Outfitters, Toys and China Shop and Mock's Fish Shop. New shops were built and opened about 1906, some incorporated into The Royal London Hotel. Some traders reopened after the fire.

Starting on the corner with Fore Street was The London Hotel.

On the New Street side, part of the building was a shop. In 1838, J. Lake, Booking Office. In 1889, John Lake, was a Cab Proprietor also in 1890 he was a posting livery stables and mail contractor. He also had a shop in Fore Street. In December 1893 the Bristol and Devon Stores, moved from the south side of New Street, and had a new shop front put in this part of the London Hotel. Some time later it became two Shops, which we will call 1 and 2.

1   Mr. R. Mock and Son, Fishmongers, listed in Kelly's Directory as Fore Street in 1906, Telephone Number 6. As this shop was near the corner with Fore Street it must have been here. By 1910 his address was 'New Street'. Leslie Mock, Fishmonger to 1952. Archie Abbott was manager of the shop for many years. We also have the name The Bargain Shop in May 1970, possibly here. By the early 1980s it was The London Hotel and Restaurant. In 1986 onwards it became one shop again.

2   After Lake's, in 1906, it was a Toy and China Shop, we have not been able to find the name for this business. This was followed by Mrs. E. Evershed, Needlework. She opened a branch here in addition to her London Studio, trading in 1919 until at 1939 when she moved to Fore Street. Mr. Pidsley, Estate Agent and Booking Office in the late 1930s, after being in Myrtle House in the High Street in 1902 and Fore Street in 1919. The next name we have is Connole, Rickeard and Green in 1926, Land and Estate Agents, Auctioneers, Surveyors and Architects. Also have a reference for 1928, Cathcart and Cathcart, Estate Agents. By 1936, it was Mr. Van Allen who was still trading in the 1940s.
The next reference for this site is GWENDOLYN MAY, Ladies Hairdressers in November 1940, and still there in 1956. In the early 1970s it was a London Hotel Bar with the entrance door on the corner with Fore Street. By the 1980s it had become The Corner Restaurant.

In 1986 part of the London Hotel was rebuilt. The shops were rebuilt as one corner unit, with the door on the corner with Fore Street, opening as FREEMAN HARDY WILLIS, a shoe shop. It has now changed to STEAD and SIMPSON, Footwear.

1st December, 1984

Coventry House.

Part of the time it was two shops with flats and offices on the first floor. The offices included: Sidmouth Fuel Control Office, and Food Traders Section in 1947 and 1951.
The two shop premises were John Opie, Men's Outfitters, 1889, by 1890 OPIE'S Outfitters and Hatters to 1897. Mr. EVANS, Outfitters, 1897 -1906. and Mrs. Elizabeth CASSON 1893, Grocer to 1906. It then became one shop. George F. TRUSCOTT, Jeweller and Watchmaker. In 1930 Truscott and Mountstephen. In 1935, A. J. MOUNTSTEPHEN.
Changed back to two shops in about 1947. Mountstephen's on the right side Mr. Eric G. CASTLE, Photographer on the left until 1968 when he was followed by a Travel Agents, Mr. Williams, later to become SIDMOUTH TRAVEL AGENCY to October 1970, when they moved to Fore Street. The two shops were combined to make one large shop, A. J. MOUNTSTEPHEN, Jewellers, Watchmakers and Goldsmiths in November 1970.

We now reach the last premises before Old Fore Street.

Taken in front of Pepperell's, corner of Old Fore Street, New Street

JAMES PEPPERELL,

Belle Vue Dairy,

MARKET PLACE, SIDMOUTH.

MILK, &c., DELIVERED DAILY.

Devonshire Cream.

Cream-Cheese.

Special Milk for
Invalids and Infants.

Devonshire Cream,
Fresh Butter, &c.,
sent
per Parcels Post
to all parts.

PURE SEPARATED CREAM.

WEEKLY HAMPERS.

PURE HONEY GATHERED FROM THE MOORS.

Reference for this corner, Mortimore to November 1867. Succeeded by Charles Webber, Chemist 1873, 1880. Then N. B. Penberthy, Drug and Patent Medicine Warehouse, 1883 - 1897. This was probably on this corner as an advertisement says 'Market Place'.

The shop door is on the corner of the building. We have a reference for a shop called THE DOME, Mr. Haycock, trading in plants and fruits, he also had a Conservatory. The business probably changed to Mr. Berwick for a time. Mr. James Pepperell bought the corner site in 1883, rebuilt and opened in 1885 as PEPPERELL DAIRY until 1919. Then the Martin family ran the dairy for many years, Walter Martin and Son, The BELLE VUE DAIRY, closing in December 1974. Change of trade to Ladies Fashions MADAME LEAVESLEY 1975.

Crossing over to the other side of New Street, starting again at Fore Street. We have not been able to check the correct location or names or the trade for each of the shops that were here before they were closed in 1957.

The shop on the corner was occupied by Mr. Richard Stone, Grocer 1816 . Edwin Venman, Grocer, Glass and China dealer in 1851 to 1870, they were also agents for Uffculme's Ale and Porter. George Passmore 1874, in April 1875 passed business to John Hutchings, China shop. Next as DEVON and BRISTOL SUPPLY STORES, W. C. Symes was proprietor in 1892. It then became, SYMES and Co, Grocer, in 1893, in the December they were to move into part of the newly altered London Hotel. J. H. Stevens, Poulterer, Greengrocer, Fruit and Flowers 1897 - 1910. The next date which we have is 1923, STAR SUPPLY STORES and STAR TEA Co. Next it changed to INTERNATIONAL STORES in 1936.

(1)   In 1891 there was Mrs. Sarah Payton, Lace maker with an assistant lace maker, and a boy in the shop, later a reference which we have is an 1866 advertisement for a Mrs. Radford, Lace dealer, advertising the shop 'to let' in June 1881. We have no more details until a E. A. Sellek, Flowers in 1914. Miss A. Steptoe, Dresses 1914 -1935. A reference for a Butchers, either a Mr. Gooding or a Mr. J. Burgoyne, 1919 -1920. The next reference is for Fido' Finch sports and sweet shop in the 1930s.

(2)   John Tedbury, Saddler and Harness maker in 1851 was still here in 1857. Mr. James Bennett, Saddler in 1859 (Deceased 1879) was succeeded by Harry Finch, Saddler. George Finch in 1926. In March 1939. Kirkpatrick - Smith, Electrical Engineers to about 1949. They may also have been called South West Electric around 1947. Then Mr. and Mrs. Stanley, Artistic and Fancy goods in 1952. The THREE SISTERS, Wool shop, earliest date 1958. still here in 1963. The last shopkeeper here may have been Mr. Locke, Antiques, (or Allan's wool shop). He then had Allan's wool shop in Fore Street, in the 1980s.

All these small shops were extensively altered into one premises to be The MIDLAND BANK, opening in May 1959. Entrance in Fore Street. Now renamed HSBC, in 1999.

3.   Between 1889 and 1893, Daniel Robertson, Tobacconist and Toys. Then he moved to Fore Street. Next names, Mr. Horatio Fenner then Mr. Russell, Tobacconist and toy dealer, in 1897. Mrs. Annie EDGCOMBE, Tobacco 1914 - 1926. D. A. Chilcott, 1937. C. H Powlesland, Tobacconist, still trading here in 1939. The SPINNING WHEEL, Wool shop, in the 1940s - 1950s. Changed to Estate Agents when GRAHAM and COMBES moved from Old Fore Street in the mid 1960s, staying until 1980. It next became HARLEQUIN, Ladies fancy goods. From the inside of the shop when the light is right angle one could still just make out the word 'Tobacconist' on the plate glass window on the left hand side of the window (1996). Shop closed in March 1996 reopened with new shopkeeper for a short time, closing shortly afterwards. In February 1997 there were alterations to the shop front, making a new front door to the flat over the shop on the left hand side. The shop opened as SIDMOUTH OUTDOOR Co. and now changed to SIDMOUTH SHOE Co.

The next part of this row of buildings was a double fronted house around 1826. Sometime later this was made into two shops.

4   In 1883 Bridgeman, Shoes, to 1893. This was followed by Alfred Buxton, Public Benefit and Boot Supplies in 1897 to the early 1900s. We have the name Cornelius Sydney Harris, Shoes, dates for 1910 and 1914. BRISTOL BOOT Co., in 1919. M. C. Councell, Boot and Shoes to 1926. The next reference we have is for My Lady Shop 1935 - 1939. Then to TROULAN'S, Opticians in 1947 - 1968. This was followed by DOLLOND and AITCHISON, also Opticians who were there until the 1970s. The shop was empty for a short time. Refurbished and opened by Miss J. Creeke in 1975. Traded as the LANTERN SHOP, Art, China, Pictures, Lamp shades, closed in 1997. New trade PURRFECT, Cat accessories shop opened in 1998 closing in September 2001. In November, proprietors Barry Hemmings, open as EMILY Chocolat, selling Belgian Chocolates.

The Summerland by the Sea, 1922

Bristol Boot Co.,
M. C. COUNCELL

TOP VALUE
—— IN ——
FOOTWEAR
for all Seasons

NEW STREET,
SIDMOUTH

5. The last shop before the Market Building was Mr. Thomas RUSSELL, Baker & Confectioner around 1850. Mr. C. Russell in 1877. In 1902 we have a reference for a Mrs. Caroline Russell and Toby Russell, Bakers. Mr. Peter HILL, Baker about 1914. In 1925 Mr. Carl PALK and his wife bought and extended the business, and with bread deliveries by bike. Then a motorcycle with a box attached, and progressing to a van. The early deliveries were only around the town, and then extending further around Sidmouth. The Name changed to PALK & SON. Mr. Carl Palk died suddenly in 1934, and his wife Kathleen conveyed the business to her son, Eric. After the war he extended the business to over 1000 customers a day. A new modern bakery was built in a cottage in Dove Lane, and a new shop window was put in, and interior alterations to the shop, in the early 1950s. In 1962 the business was sold and became GOODBOY'S, they were still trading in 1968. It then became STEPHENS BAKERY until December 1986. The shop ended trading as Bakers and was closed until December 1988. The premises then became THE LANTERN SHOP GALLERY.

Delivering Bread for P. Hill

Kirkpatrick - Smith

RADIO and ELECTRICAL ENGINEERS

New Street

Sidmouth

Distinctive Modern and Period Lighting Fittings

Exclusive Lampshades

Electrical Appliances and Radio of the Highest Quality

Your Murphy Dealer
Sidmouth's Finest Radio Repair Service

A. E. BUXTON,
NEW STREET, SIDMOUTH.

PUBLIC BENEFIT BOOT SUPPLY

TRIED AND PROVED

WE MOVE WITH THE TIMES.
Specialities—Special Manufactured Goods, "The Piccadilly" and "The Baronet."

Go to **J. OPIE'S**
NEW STREET, SIDMOUTH,

FOR UP-TO-DATE-CLOTHING,
HATS, TIES, ETC.,

Whose Stock is now replete with the

Latest Styles and Patterns
for the Season.

Appointed Agent for Kino's
SPECIAL TROUSERS TO MEASURE AT 13/6,
A CHOICE SELECTION.

OLD FORE STREET, EAST SIDE

We have references for the following shops, but have not been able to accurately locate them. The Post Office, Mr. George Turner, Post Master, 1835-1838. Lewis Sommervill, Grocer in 1851. William Troake, shopkeeper, Grocer and toy maker in 1856-1879. Robert Hart, Lace Maker in 1866, in November 1869 the house furnishing, shop counters together with a pony and cart were for sale. W. Lake, Gents Outfitters in 1897. J. Bickley opened a Butchers shop in February 1897. George Medhurst, agent for Singer Sewing Machine Co. in 1890. Daniel James, Bootmaker and shopkeeper, in 1870. Samuel Squire Gimblett, Boot and shoes, 1878, also had a shop in Exeter. Charles Smith, shopkeeper 1919. Jenny Diver, Decorations for the Home, 1955-1958.

Starting at the end of the High Street, on the East side. The first buildings are the backs of the first four, Fore Street shops. (See Fore Street.) At various times these buildings have also been small individual shops, opening onto Old Fore Street, Mr. R J Russell in 1946. VALET CLEANERS. Mr. and Mrs. P. G. Cooper 1946-1949, They had a quick dry cleaners in Russell Street. Mr. Cooper MODEL SUPPLIES, Model Railways 1950s and now the back entrances to the shops in Fore Street, Choices and Threshers.

M. Ankins

Old Fore Street, 1983

We now come to the back entrance of what is now the Black Horse Inn. Next to the Inn was a row of cottages, which date to about 1900, extending down to Cross Lane. We have a reference for William Sanders and Son, Cabinet Maker his son was a Carpenter in 1856. All the cottages were demolished and a new building was built and became, Sanders, Furniture, Undertakers, Estate Agents. On the first floor and at the back of the shop were the carpenters workshops, with the entrance through double doors in Cross Lane. Closed in about 1953.

Mates Guide

Empty for a time before REGINALD LEONARD bought the shop in February 1955. Soft Furnishings until mid 1960s.

It was then made into five small shops on the ground floor.

6.   This is the first floor over the ground floor shops becoming number 6. ANTONIS, (Newbury) Hairdresser in the mid 1960s to 1970s. It next became HAIRFLAIR. Changed to KITCHEN DESIGN in May 1988 and TEA ROOMS in 1991. Next TRULY SCRUMPTIOUS, tea rooms. In April 2001 taken over by Lisa Jameson and Neil Holland. TRULY SCRUMPTIOUS COFFEE BAR.

5.   In 1961, THE LIZZARD, Mr. Selley, Coffee shop. Next was HAYDEE, Mrs. Curtis 1967. S. E. S. Stationers, Records. 1972, also on the first floor in 1974, closing down in 1981 on moving into the High Street. Empty in 1983. Maureen Goodland opened, FRILLS, Soft furnishings and Haberdashery, in 1988.

4.   ALLANS, Wool before, OPENSHAW, Soft furnishings 1967. Next a SWEET Shop, H. Denies about 1967. Empty 1983. Next ANTIQUE and GOLD BUYING CENTRE closing in September 1988. GALLERY 21, October 1990. Later taken as one shop with number 3 next door.

3.   Hairdresser Mr. John HOLLICK, in June 1967 to September 1981. Next LUDGATE GALLERY. Shop empty in 1983. FOUNDATIONS, Soft furnishings 1988. Changed to LUDGATE GALLERY in 1993. In November 1999 sold to Roger Davies. Keeping the shop name. In September 2000, a new trade, C C S COM. Mobile Phone Shop, closing in August 2001.

1907

2.	B. and M. CLEMENTS, Sport Wear. Next TIBBLES (Birmingham Ltd.) 1960s. Next STAG, Mr. R. Carton, Men's Outfitters 1981. THE CORNISH WOOLLEN Shop, Mr John Stevens, 1988. It then changed to LEISURETIME in August 1989. New trade in May 1997, HEAVERS, Home Improvements.

1.	GILBEY J. ELLIS, Fancy Goods, Pictures, to October 1963. G. R. MOCK, Fish Shop in 1967. BLACKBIRD, Shoes mid 1970s. LIMELIGHT, Shoes, Mr. Burral to 1983. We believe this property was then empty until 1986, when Mr Ross and Margaret Denver opened as No 1 BY DESIGN, Essentially Silver.

J. Ankins

June 1988, Old Fore Street

We now can cross over Cross Lane, sometimes called Trumps Lane, details see Fore Street.

On the corner there were four small cottages. In January 1875 these were advertised as dilapidated cottages for sale. One was bought by Mr Bitter, the occupier for £350. The three adjoining cottages were bought by Mr. Trump. for £365. Rebuilt to become Cosmopolitan House.

J. Ankins

1983, Trumps Despatch Departmennt

    The Back of Cosmopolitan House was Trumps Stores, Dispatch Departments, all inward goods were unloaded, and all their own delivery vans loaded from here. Wine bottling was done in the first part of the ground floor. They bought the wine in large wooden barrels and the wine was put into bottles and labelled with Trumps own labels. This was all done by hand. The centre section was the dispatch entrance and the end section was the Coffee Blending department were the coffee beans were roasted. The extractor fan in the window sent the coffee smells all along Old Fore Street.

In 1983 converted into three units, with offices on the first floor. Opened as shops in 1984.

First shop next to Cross Lane was, JONCRAFT, John Curtis, Toys, May 1984. ROBERT CRISP, Picture Frames, 1987 - 1989. SPORTING IMAGES, Hairdressers opened in July 1990.
NATIONAL TRUST July 1984.

LITTLE CHARACTERS, Children clothes, they were here from April 1984 until April 1987, when they moved to Church Street. The shop was then amalgamated into The NATIONAL TRUST shop.

Next shop down was TRUMPS, Bakers from about 1875. They also had a confectionery counter in the main shop, in Fore Street. They did all their own baking and the smell of fresh baking in the early morning was followed by the coffee blending. In 1983 changing to SUE'S PANTRY, Bakers. Closing in January 2001.

The Summerland by the Sea

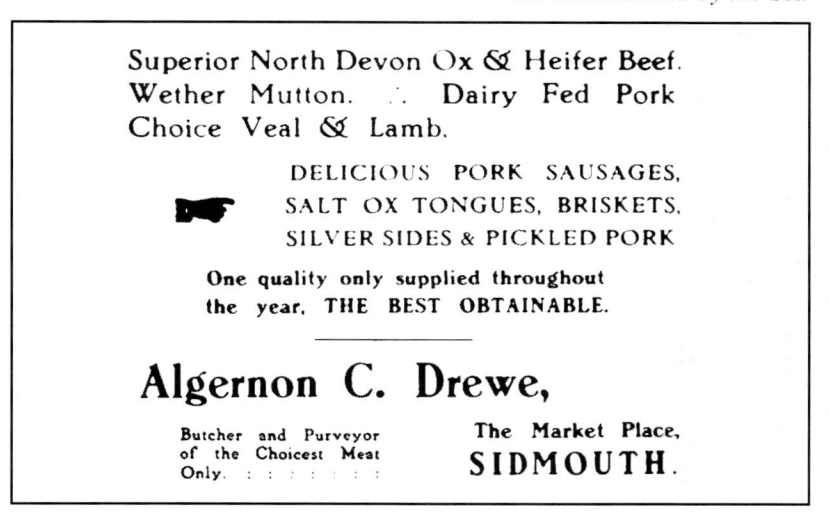

Superior North Devon Ox & Heifer Beef.
Wether Mutton. ∴ Dairy Fed Pork
Choice Veal & Lamb.

DELICIOUS PORK SAUSAGES,
SALT OX TONGUES, BRISKETS,
SILVER SIDES & PICKLED PORK

One quality only supplied throughout
the year. THE BEST OBTAINABLE.

Algernon C. Drewe,

Butcher and Purveyor
of the Choicest Meat
Only. : : : : : :

The Market Place,
SIDMOUTH.

1922

On down the road, a reference for Albion House, which we believe is this property. As far as we know this was built by Mr. Albert Maeer. It then became a Butchers shop. Names for this site, Albert Maeer, 1883. I Skinner, 1896. Algernon Cecil Drewe in 1897. By 1926, H. W. DREWE and SON to 1968. The ground floor was altered and a new shop front put in by Mr. and Mrs. Nigel Ruddle. November 1970 became The GAYE SHOP Gifts, China, etc. and now called SIDMOUTH GIFTS.

On the corner with New Street was Belle Vue Dairy. Now Madame Leavesley. (See New Street).

Wallpaper and Paints Supply Store.   House Decorators

LEASK & CO,
(Late H. F. Sellek)

Members of the N.F.M.P.

OLD FORE STREET, SIDMOUTH.

———o———

Agents for :
Winsor & Newton Artist Colours.

———o———

Telephone **225**.

Works : Sellek's Yard, Sid Place.

O. F. (Stengel & Co)

Post Mark 1931   Pepperell Dairy, Bottom Old Fore Street

NETTOYAGE A SEC

GOOD DRY CLEANING IS NOW, MORE THAN EVER BEFORE, ESSENTIAL TO ALL

R E G N K L A D E R S   &   P R E S E N N I N G S F A B R I K S

The Valet
(P. G. COOPER).
Cleaners
Old Fore Street, Sidmouth

Always have and will continue, to offer the finest and Best Service in the District.

The difference is that every garment is
VALET PRESSED
by a Pioneer of the Valet Service in the U.K. (London 1920) and expert users of the very first English make steam Tailor Presses (1924).

And again the FIRST
QUICK DRY CLEANERS
(Trichlorethyline) 1929.

In our OWN WORKS at :—RUSSELL STREET, SIDMOUTH

The **VALET** *for Satisfaction*

TRICOTAGE FABRIEKEN

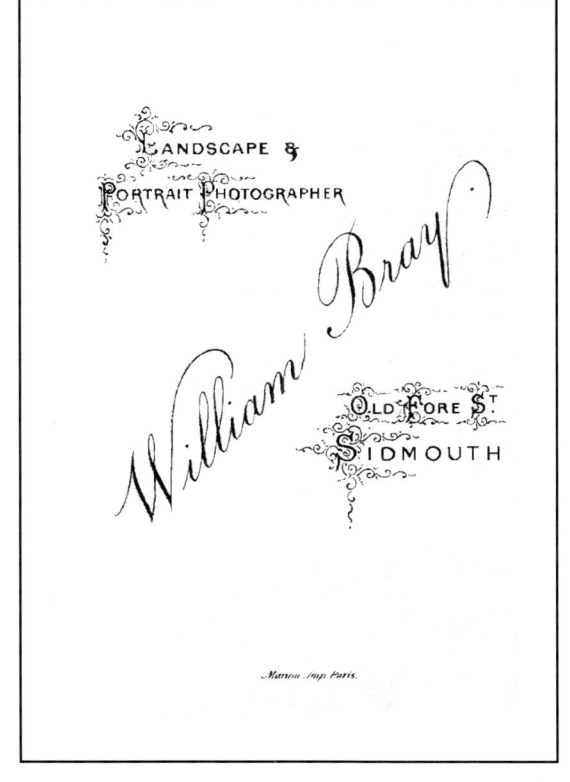

R E G N F R A K K E F A B R I K E N

Landscape & Portrait Photographer

William Bray

Old Fore St. Sidmouth

Marion Imp Paris.

107

OLD FORE STREET, WEST SIDE

Returning to the top end of Old Fore Street we can now go down the west side, past the entrance to the back of the first shops. In here was a tall building and large double gates to the Town Brewery. After the Brewery closed, part of the building was used by Sanders as curtains and upholstery workrooms and the storage for carpets. Now been rebuilt as town houses, Lennards Court and Lakes Court.

The first shop on corner was Mrs. EVERSHED, Church and Decorative Needlework. Moved to here from New Street about 1936. Next it became PAWLYNS, Dresses, Gowns, opened in April 1948, still trading under this name today.

THE SHIP INN, is one of the oldest buildings in the town. It was reputed to have been built in 1350 and it may have been a monastery, before becoming an Inn.

A restaurant was incorporated and part of the Inn was made into a small shop. In 1981 it was FOLLYS, nearly new clothes. Then in 1982, there was an Antiques Centre. In 1983, a HOT FOOD TAKE AWAY, selling fish and chips etc,.

The next property, after the Inn there was a Mr. Frederick Mitchell, Painter and Glazier in Fore Street in 1850 and a Plumber in 1866. Frederick Mitchell, Painters, Paperhangers to about 1878. In 1879 Mrs. C. MITCHELL and SON, furniture brokers were here. By 1893 Mr. Harry F. SELLEK, Painter, although the name Mitchell is still there in 1897. It then became LEASK and Co. Painters, Wallpaper 1934-1955. GRAHAM and COMBES, Estate Agents, Painters and Decorators, until they moved to New Street in 1960. The next reference is for La BOUTIQUE, Mrs Carol Beanland. 1975 the name changed to SAFFRON, which Carol ran with her husband, Julian until 1981. Then it became PICTURES and PASTIMES. This was a double fronted shop, which by 1991 had been split into two shops. The lower shop, becoming PANACHE, by 1997. Line dancing was becoming popular so Doreen Freeman starting selling the clothing and accessories in the shop.

Next was the entrance, through an archway to the OLD MANOR YARD, workshops stores etc. The entrance from the road had two large wooden doors in the archway, there were two large stones one on each side to keep the cart wheels from rubbing the doors as they went in and out of the yard. The name Joseph Godfrey, Plumbers may have been here in 1852-1890. In 1850. Mr Abraham Lake founder of the business LAKE and SONS, with Warehouse and Stores on the corner of East Street and Gas House Lane (Ham Lane), now part of the car park. The Business was Plumbing, Gas Fitters, Range Manufacturer, 'The Devon Herald Ranges' and general Smiths, (not horse shoeing). In 1880 he opened his shop here in Old Fore Street, accommodation was over the shop. The firm took over all the Manor Yard next to the shop about 1891. There was a Carpenters Shop, Plumbers and Paint Store. Also a saw pit in the corner of the yard. The Foreman Carpenter lived over the shop next door.

Mr. A. Lake had seven sons who all spent some time with the firm.

The firm operated the first telephone Exchange, The Bell Telephone Company. This accounts for Mr. Lake's Telephone number '1'. This was in a room at the back of the shop, in the night someone had to come downstairs to plug in the line to connect to the subscriber. The National Telephone Company opened the first Telephone Exchange here in Sidmouth in 1896. In the 1899-1900 NTC Telephone Directory, it lists sixteen lines on the Sidmouth exchange. Line No. 1 was the Call Office. Mr. Lake's National number changed to '3'. By 1906 the exchange had moved to Church Street.

Mr. Tom Lake ran the shop and plumbing business here until they closded in 1983.

The shop then became MARINERS, Estate Agents in November 1984. About 1988 it changed to COOKSLEY MARINERS and in 1994 a new business, CURTAIN and FABRIC SHOP, Closing down in May 1996. In June a charity shop SUE RYDER moved from the old gas showrooms. Closing in 1997. In 1998 The Handmade lace shop moved into here from Fore Street and became THE ROMANTIC ENGLISHWOMAN, In September 1999 the name was changed to FOREVER ENGLAND.

At the back of the shop the yard and workshops were cleared and flats where then built in 1989 and now called LAKES COURT.

J. Ankins

1960, County Steam Laundry and Lakes

Baskerville House.

This was a Printers, W. COOK, here in 1901, he may have been earlier, to 1905. SID VALE PRESS and PRINTING Co. Mr. Tucker, 1919-1952. COUNTY STEAM LAUNDRY in the 1950s. Changed to GREENFINGERS, Garden shop, Mr. R. A. Artingstall, in October 1960. Then to TUDOR AMETHYST, Jewellery in 1972, Semi precious gem stones. End of November 2000 closed and PUDDLEDUCKS, moved into here from their shop next door.

Fitzalan House.

In 1902 the shop, house and yard were for sale. The first reference which we have found is W. Passmore in 1925 (possibly here much earlier). Changing to Mr. W. J. BARBER, Watchmaker and Jeweller, who was also an agent for Decca Gramophones, advertised 'with over 1,000 records in stock', 1930s. Mr. C. WOOD, Jeweller, 1947. Empty in 1987. In 1988 it became PUDDLEDUCKS, Toys and Games, Teddy Bears. Closing November 2000, as they moved up the road to the shop next door. Anne Barratt opened as FITZALAN GEMS.

Next down the road, the first date as a shop is for Mr. E. J. Staples, Arts and Crafts 1939-1952. Ruth's Cake Shop 1967-1978. Then to an Opticians, BEDFORD JOHNS when they moved from Salcombe Road in the 1980s. Changed to BOOTS, OPTICIANS, in March 1987, and to BATEMANS OPTICIANS in November 1996.

Windsor House.

Possible that in 1879, a Mrs. Stone, refreshment rooms and shopkeeper. The property was bought by Mr. Bray in December 1880. Bray and Son 1890. China and Antiques. Brays Café in the 1930s-1940s. Then Windsor Café and Guest House. To White Horses in the 1960s. Sambati Café 1990s. In the 1990s WHITE HORSE CAFÉ and TAKE AWAY.

Next a small shop with the old shop window and step up to the door. Miss Ethel Bolt, Dress maker, in 1919. A Sweet shop in the 1930-1935. Mr. H. Week, Children's Outfitters 1937-1950s. Vivienne 1960-1963. Bamber or Raberr?, Dresses 1975. THE LITTLE SHOP. In 1982, SEFTON Antiques for Country Houses. Then as FORTUNES, Noel and Rosemary Power, opened in March 1990, Astrology, Clairvoyant to 1991. Changed again to The LITTLE SHOP Antiques, and to The Old Curiosity Shop in 1997.

Another small fronted shop with the original bow fronted shop window and steps up to the shop door. The first reference for here is, Wright-Luff, The Chintz Shop. Then Thomas Joseph BUSSELL, Picture Frames, China 1906-1939, followed by Mr. E, HYATT Antiques 1940s to 1984. Empty 1984. All the interior altered to reopen with a new name, Regency House, by Miss J, Creeke in June 1985. The LITTLE LANTERN SHOP, Pictures, Lamp Shades. Closing in February 1988 and moving to New Street. Empty again to March 1989, then reopened as ALEXANDER THE GRATES, Fireplaces, to November 1989.

Next RICHFIELDS, Body Care 1990 to June 1991. Next Gina Crosthwaite opened in August 1993. BIJOU Designer Giftware. In 1997 REGENCY HOUSE BOOKS.

Sidmouth and District Directory

**THE DON,
OLD FORE STREET,**

*Tobacconists, Confectioners
and Stationers.*

We Buy with care, so our Goods are always of Best Value and Reliable. We give personal attention in selling so Customers can depend on
COURTESY, PROMPTNESS & CONSIDERATION.

MISSES TAYLOR & BOND.

1937

Banwell House

This was listed as apartments, Mr. George Smith in 1902, he was in Cambridge Villas before this. Mr. Charles Smith, Confectioner, 1919 - 1923. Next THE DON, Misses Taylor and Bond, Confectionery and Stationery, 1935-1939. Sweets and Tobacco in 1940, two of the people who ran it were, Bert Bess and John Burgoyne. Change of trade to ARMBANDS, Jewellers in 1988. ORMANDY'S JEWELLERS, Mr. Alan Ormandy, closing in September 2001.

Honiton Lace Shop (Established 1780). In 1852. Stephen Hayman, Lace Manufacturers, listed as 'near the Market', and Mrs. Caroline Hayman in 1856 as Market Place, and in 1866 as on the Esplanade. in 1878 as Prospect Place. This shop has a bay window standing out from the front of the building. Mrs. Mary N. Barnard, listed as in the Market Place in 1890, in 1893 as Old Fore Street, by 1925 Miss Hannah Barnard. On the fascia board above the window there was one word BARNARD into the mid 1960s. The first change of trade for this small shop was when Mr. Brian BAGWELL Estate Agents opened, they were here to 1988. Changed to BRISTOL and WEST Property Services in June 1987. WHITEHOUSE, Estate Agents to 1994. New trade, HONEY POT Gift shop, closed 1995. GEMINI, Gifts and Antiques in 1997. Closed for a time until early 1999 and opened as, STATE OF THE ART, closing down in October 2000. Opened in April 2001 as HEALTHYBITZ, Magnetic therapy products, having moved from their shop in the High Street.

> **M. N. Barnard,**
>
> **HONITON LACE MANUFACTURER**
>
> Mrs. BARNARDS GRANDMOTHER (Mrs Nicholls) made a special Pattern for H.R.H. the Dutchess of Kent, and H.R.H. Princess Victoria in the yaar 1830
>
> Mrs. BARNARDS MOTHER (Mrs. Hayman) made the Wedding Lace for H.R.H. Princess Christina, and Pocket Handkerchief for H.R.H. Princess Louise.
>
> **Old Fore Street, SIDMOUTH**
>
> ESTABLISHED 1780.

1907

ANCHOR INN. (Including The Anchor Yard).

The Inn is a large building compared with the rest of the row of shops and is set back from the line of the others, with a small alley way to the back of the building by the neighbouring shop, and an entrance with double doors through an archway on the south side leading to the yard at the back with various outbuildings. There also used to be a pathway to Church Lane and this closed in December 1966.

The next shops to Church Street are listed under the Market Place.

MARKET PLACE

Sidmouth and District Directory

Are you fond of Reading?

FRESH SUPPLIES

of POPULAR FICTION to suit all tastes are received regularly from our LONDON WHOLESALERS.

COME & CHOOSE

your next book from our shelves.

BOOKLAND
— FOR BOOKS —
Market Place, SIDMOUTH

An immensely popular idea.

1837

Starting at the end of Old Fore Street. After the archway to the back of the Anchor Inn, the shops stand out from the line of the Inn. This may have been one shop with Mr. Lethaby next door. In about 1800 this was a Coffee Tavern. This became a shop by 1835, John Harvey, Stationers, BOOKLAND with a Circulating Library. In 1836 it was also the Bridport Branch

Bank, Samuel and Walter Eustace Gundry, Mr. Harvey was the manager. He was also agent for County Fire & Provident Life Offices, here to about 1866 when it was under the name Miss Elizabeth Harvey, Stationers. The next reference, which we have is for Mr. Davis, Stationers, also for The Perth Dye Works in 1905. Mr. R. Tucker, 1914-1919. Shop then changed to MAY SMITH, Greengrocer, Florist in the early 1920s to the 1970s. SPINDELLS in 1978. JUST JOY, Flowers in 1981 to September 1988. Changing to ANNIES, Cane and Basketware.

Mr. Richard LETHABY, Printers and Books here in 1858 with a Circulating Library by 1890. The Sidmouth Journal and Directory was published monthly, Miss E. LETHABY, Wool and Fancy goods in 1873. Mrs. Lethaby to February 1904. The next trade which we can find for this site is of a Mr. and Mrs. CROSS, Fishmonger's. Then MAC FISHERIES, with the first date which we have is 1926, they were here until 1979. Then there was a change of trade to Wines and Spirits, VICTORIA WINE, staying to 7th February 1999. This had the same owners, First Quench, as Thresher's, Wine shop in Fore Street. On September 20th Rodds, Men's Outfitters moved here from Fore Street.

Mr. Arthur Richard Tremlett, Fish and Chip shop around 1910, and probably a Grocers as well. The next business here may have been Burgoyne's, High Class Ladies and Gent's Hairdressing Saloons in 1922. Then BURGOYNE, Greengrocer to Percy BARON, Greengrocer in the late 1920s. He had a Fruit and Vegetable Nursery in Woolbrook near Stowford. Then NANCY BARONS to 1968 when Mr and Mrs. Brown took over. Mrs. Brown (Florrie) first worked in the shop and then managed it for many years before she and her husband took it over. Then Mr Chalmers. The shop name still remained, BARONS until November 1986 when they moved to Fore Street. It then became SWEET TEMPTATIONS in May 1987.

Mr. John WEEKES opened a new shop, Boot and Shoes, here in May 1894 to about 1923. Change of trade to Ironmonger, Mr. ROWE. Next, George E. ELKINS, Ladies and Gentleman's Highclass Footwear Establishment. 1926-1978. The premises then became GLIDDON & SON, Ironmongers, with their other shop on the corner with Church Street.

We cross over Church Street to the corner site. A large two storey block of houses.

At the back of this block were cottages and yard. Fields had the large yard with a high wood fence along the South side with an entrance by the alley way from the Market Place. The main way in for carts etc. was from the sea front at the side of the Marlborough. At the west end of the yard was part of the Baths, on the Esplanade, with an open air sea water bath. Now all built on as town houses. There were three small cottages, some with their own wells for water, now part of the shop.

In 1880 as two Dwelling Houses and one Four Room Cottage were for sale. The cottage was occupied by Mr. John Tapley. The sale had a poor attendance, Lot 1 only one bid of £950, and therefore no sale was made. Lot 2 started at £550 and reached £780. This was still below the reserved price so again no sale was made.

The first house (Lot 1) was facing the market Place next to the alley way to the back of the buildings. On the ground floor there was a spacious shop with large plate glass windows. At the time of sale it was divided into two shops on the ground floor, one shop was Mr. Hugh TALBOT in 1850, Dispensing and Family Chemist. After him it may have been Charles F WEBBER, dispensing druggist, in 1878.

The other shop (lot 2) Mr. Frank, BARNARD, Sidmouth CLOTHING ESTABLISHMENT, Hatter, Outfitters, with warerooms, coal house, and covered yard with side and back entrances, here in 1877, still advertising in 1880.

One these buildings was a Bank, in about the mid 1880s. (Sidmouth had its own bank notes), One of the cottages was Wicks Draper around 1866-1870s. However, we have not found the exact location for these businesses.

The next house (lot 2) was a double fronted house. The first date which we have found is 1852. This became a Post Office and Stationers, Mr. Reuben Barratt, Postmaster. By 1856, Mrs. Georgina Barratt. In 1882, Mrs. Lucy Rainger, Postmistress. The Post Office closed in 1887 reopening in Fore Street.

Stockport House.
1.   In 1810. William Gale, Linen draper, William Gale and Son, in 1930. Also Mary Gale, Milliner and dress maker. W. N. Gale, Linen draper and Milliner in 1836. Alfred W. May, Draper, in 1878. Changed in 1889, to Henry W. MACKENZIE, Hairdresser, Perfumer and Tobacco, to 1906. Gilbert Edgar ORMAN, Hairdresser and Wigmaker, An advertisement mentioned a 'Sidmouth Toilet Club'. By 1906 he had moved to Church Street.

2/3   Matthew HALL, Silk and Linen Drapers in 1810, and also an agent for West of England and South Wales District Bank, also a Silk Mercer by 1836. Changed to Mr. FIELD, in 1893 he also had Number 3. The shop sold mainly ladies clothes, as the men's shop was in Fore Street. By 1896 Mr. John Field had Number 4 as well. Around 1914, Number 1 was also incorporated into the shop. In February 1978 the business was bought by C. Spores, but trading was still under the name FIELDS. The last change has incorporated one more shop in Church Street, last known as The Vine in 1995, at the bottom of Church Street.

Mr. Santer started his own grocery business after working in Trumps Stores, in one of these shops, before moving to the High Street in 1939.

Next towards the sea front. This was the site of The ANCHOR INN until 1805 when it was demolished. There is a pathway between the shops. Over the pathway the first floors were joined by a covered passage. In November 1913 a new shop was built for Mr. L. Field, Furniture Shop. Later to change to SUZANNE, Florist. The first floor over the shop has had various trades. The covered passage has now been taken down.

We are now in Prospect Place.

The Duke of Marlborough Hotel, in recent years as The Marlborough. This has a small room with a entrance on the market side and in the 1980s it housed a slot machine arcade. In February 1993 it became, ETHNIC INFLUENCE, which closed in 1998.

We will cross over the road and walk back towards the Market Place.

On the corner with the Esplanade was Number 3 called 'The Shed' a meeting or reading rooms in 1810. Later made into shops on the ground floor and now site of the Mocha Café. The Mocha Café which was listed as being in Fore Street and the Esplanade in 1923. Miss Hilda Grover and in 1926, Miss Constance Grover, Proprietress. By 1930 only advertised as being on the Esplanade. In 1931, it was The BIARRITZ, Restaurant, it advertised as 'Sidmouth's New Rendezvous', with a large room for hire for socials and dances, to about 1939. It then changed to the MOCHA CAFE. Still under the name, The MOCHA Restaurant today.

Mates Guide

The first reference which we have is for Number 1 Prospect Place, and this was for a Bath House. (Or Bath Rooms) Hot and Cold Shower / Baths. The name, Mrs. Roberts appears for 1836. William Bennington in 1857, Berlin and Fancy repositories. Later it was apartments.

Between the Mocha and Kings Lane, were two private houses. Sometime, late 1920s early 1930s made into a shop. THE PROSPECT SNACK BAR in the mid 1940s, and in 1950s SNACK BAR and RESTAURANT. The 1980s, an ICE CREAM PARLOUR. In May 2000 called ICE CREAM PARADISE.

The MOCHA
SIDMOUTH
also at Cathedral Close, Exeter
'Phones : Sidmouth 282
Exeter 4924

HOME-MADE GOODIES
DAINTY MEALS
COURTEOUS SERVICE
BREAD, CAKES, CHOCOLATES, CANDIES. EVERYTHING HOME-MADE

1838

We have not been able find out when it became two shops, the first reference we have is THE PROSPECT OF SIDMOUTH, in the 1970s. This became WELLINGTONS in April 1987, and then THE PROSPECT CAFE and TAKE AWAY.

Souvenir Book Hospital

RESTAURANT BIARRITZ

High-Class Caterers

ESPLANADE :: SIDMOUTH.

Sidmouth's New Rendezvous.
:: DANCING BY THE SEA. ::

First-Class Food at Moderate Charges in Modern Surroundings.

OPEN from 8 a.m. till 11 p.m.

BREAKFASTS
LUNCHEONS
TEAS
DINNERS and
SUPPERS

SPECIAL TERMS FOR PARTIES.

LARGE ROOM CAN BE HIRED for WHIST DRIVES, SOCIALS & DANCES

1931

Colin Healey

1914, Prospect Place

117

Colin Healey

1925

Sidmouth Museum

Prospect Place

We cross over Kings Lane to the shops to Dove Lane.

Sidmouth Guide

Rickwoods' Telephone 187

For all Holiday Requirements

Confectionery   Stationery   Tobacco

News   Gifts

PROSPECT PLACE, SIDMOUTH

1957

(1) This was a private house before being made into a shop on the ground floor and opening as, Mr. J. O'BRIEN and Sons, Newsagents, in the mid 1920s. A well was found inside the shop premises when renovations were taking place. It changed to RICKWOODS', Confectionery, Stationery, early 1940s. It then became the PROSPECT NEWSAGENCY.

(2) Next down the property in 1919, was called West View, Mr. Lionel Montague Tancred Purdue, Artist, and Mrs. R. A. Purdue, Fancy Repository. Changed about 1960 to a SPORTS Shop, Mr. J. R. Bloxham, and then Mr A. Burrow to December 1982. Then J. Dakers, and now Mr. Roger Faulkner. Sport and Beach equipment. In 1998 called SIDMOUTH SURF SHOP still run Mr. and Mrs. Faulkner.

Avon House was two shops.

(3) The first reference for here is W. H. NORK & CO., 1902. We have been unable to find any details or trade. In 1930s it was Sanders Estate Office, until the 1940s. The next trade here was RHENA SHOES, to October 1970. The second shop was The MARKET STREET POST OFFICE and GIFT SHOP. Mr. Martin Rabey, was Postmaster, he moved here in 1938 from Temple Street. Next Postmaster, was Mr. J. F. Passmore. After the death of Mr. Passmore, Mrs. Eileen Passmore carried on the business. In 1970, the premises were made into one shop, a new shop front and door put in. The Post Office was moved to what was the shoe shop, The old Post Office side became a Gift and Card Shop.

Mrs. Passmore died on October 31st. 1998, and her daughter Marie, took over with her husband Mr. Barry Martin. On May 6th, 2000 the Post office closed and became CARDS FOR ALL SEASONS still run by Barry and Marie.

We now are at DOVE LANE. On the south side CARINAS (See Fore Street.) On the other side, in from Fore Street, there is an entrance for the shop in Fore Street. The cottage next door was made into a shop in 1990. THE SIDMOUTH MUSIC SHOP. Next it became CANTABILE, Classical Compact Discs in 1992. Closed in January 2000. On May 9th Di Collings opened as TASTY BAGUETTE.

Next door is still a private cottage.

On the corner with Market Lane was a bakery, (shop in New Street) double doors to bakery and front door to the Flats over the shop. In 1988 made into garages for The Lantern Shop Gallery.

J. Ankins

The Market House

There was a Market Cross near the steps at the west entrance of the Market House. The first date which we have found is 1322. The cross was taken down in 1795. There are references for markets being held here in 1200, there were sheds, stalls or shops. Around 1810 there was a low brick building with a weather cock on the top.

In 1830 Parliament granted an Act for building a Commodious Market House and granting the Market dues to the Lord of the Manor. In 1839 a new building was built on the same site. In 1862 a well was dug and water pump installed for public use.

In 1903 the S.U.D.C bought the Market building from the Manor. Part of the south end of the building was made into a fire station. This was for the new horse drawn Steam Fire Engine called 'Belmont', which had been given to the town in 1902 by Mr. R. H. Wood. This also housed an escape (ladder) belonging to the U. D. C. Market stallholders used the remaining ground floor. On the first floor, which was reached from a door and stairs from an entrance in New Street, there was a large meeting room. It was used as a clubroom, Church Lads' Brigade, a Girls' Club and for Dancing classes, etc.

In August 1929, a new Market building was built. Toilets were built into each end, and the central area was for stallholders. Over the years these included, J. Field and Son, Drapers, F. B. Ford, Ian Winchester, Greengrocers, also Drew and Son, Ireland and Lewis, Butchers. Fishmongers and various other trades.

Sidmouth Herald

GLIDDON and SON
IRONMONGERS;
Sheffield House and Church Street, Sidmouth

SOLE AGENTS IN THIS DISTRICT for the celebrated
"Marmet," "Sol" and "Tan Sad"

BEST CARRIAGES NEVER DUPLICATED.
ALSO THE TOY MODELS MADE BY THESE FIRMS.
OUR BABY CARRIAGES are mostly quite unique, being designed and selected for us by experts, and are fully guaranteed.
MECCANO SETS & HORNBY TRAINS In Great Variety.
REPAIRS, RENOVATIONS & TYRING DONE ON THE PREMISES.
ALL BABY CARRIAGE ACCESSORIES IN STOCK.

March 1939

CHURCH STREET. SOUTH SIDE

Starting at the bottom of the road.

1. Mr. E. Barrett, Tailor here in 1822. Saunders, Upholsterers 1844-1870s. No other names until, Dunster's, The Wood Shop, Woodcrafts in 1937. Mr. Arthur Johnson, Antiques in the1940s. Evelyn Bailey, Corsetière, 1951. Now all part of Fields shop.

2. The first date we have found for here is 1927, Walter GALLIN & BROWN, Ladies and Gentlemen's Hairdresser when they moved to here from the other side of the road. By 1938 the name had changed to W. GALLIN. In the 1960s, PEPYS Antiques and to COPPERFIELDS, in the 1970s, Gifts Souvenirs. THE VINE in 1990. In 1995 taken into Fields Shop.

Penrhyn House
3. Mesdames ELEANOR and FRANCES, Fashion Specialist in the 1930s-1950s. Mr. and Mrs. Wilson Antiques, around the mid 1960s. VANITY FAYRE (KNIGHTS) in 1973 closing in 1991 on moving into their main shop in Fore Street. Next it became a Charity shop, SAVE THE CHILDREN opening in October 1991.

4. F. M. GLIDDONS STORES, Ironmongers, 1877. Later to a Baby carriage specialist, and Toys shop. Shop still trading with Gliddon family today.

5. Mr. J. TRIPE, Dairy about 1850. Mr. M. HOLMES, Dairy about 1883. Mr. DENNER, Dairyman, 1893-1897. Mr. and Mrs. SKINNER, Mrs. Skinner ran the shop and Mr. Arthur Skinner ran Bickwell Farm. THE MILK SHOP early 1900. Later to be called the BICKWELL VALLEY DAIRY in the 1950s. Then BICKWELL FARM DAIRY. Now THE DAIRY SHOP.

Cross over CHAPEL STREET.

Aberdeen House.
6. William SELLEK, Butcher 1866 to 1869. Samuel WHEATON, 1868 to 1894. H. B. BASTIN, 1894 to 1906. Mr. J. B. HAYMAN, Butchers, bought the business in 1907. The Hayman family still trading here today.

7.   There was an Orman, hairdresser in the Market Place in 1893. Mrs. G. E. ORMAN, Hair Specialists, early 1906-1947. R. C. JEFFERY, 1948 to 1950. R. H. SPINKS, 1951. ERIC FOYLE in the 1960s. J. HADLEY, March 1971. Change of trade, Lindsay Crosthwaite in 1980, SOMETHING SPECIAL to 1990. SOUTHWEST DISCOUNT, Jewellers open November 1990 to 1992. VENUS HAIR SALON in March 1992. Now EVELYN JONES Hair Salon

Mates 1907 Guide Book

G. E. ORMAN,

Hair Specialist and Chiropodist.

Send sample of Hair for Microscopic Examination and Postal Order **2/9** for trial bottle of
Orman's Celebrated Hair Lotion.
Numerous Testimonials.

CHURCH STREET, SIDMOUTH.

8.   John Webber, Bakers around 1822 to 1841. William Russell. Baker and Confectioner 1842 to about 1883. John Squire here in 1887-1889. Alfred WOODLEY, STEAM BAKER, here by 1904. This was followed by William HAYMAN in 1910. P SELWYN until April 1950. Now WHITE'S BAKERY, SIDMOUTH.

9.   James LASHBROOK and sons. Tailor around 1910 -1945. Mr L. T. STAMP, Cycles 1945 to 1968. Next a change of trade, JOAN'S WOOL SHOP, J. Marriott until 1991. TAM

Marketing, Cleaning Products, November 1992. To PHOENIX DESIGN, Interiors Fabric Specialist July 1993. In 1999 SID SOFT, Computer Spares & Repairs.

10.   We have found the name, Mr. Lloyd for this site around 1901-1914, but no trade details. The National Telephone Co. had moved from Old Fore Street by 1906. In 1925 the name changed to Sidmouth Telephone Exchange. In 1931 a new switchboard was introduced and the exchange moved to Radway Road. The next name and trade we have is Ralph Wood, furniture Dealer around 1926. The next name which we have is Cyril Huggett, Antique Dealer in 1930, and Mr. W. J. MARTIN, Secondhand dealer about 1940, and later a sweet shop in 1941. In March 1970, Frank Haylet opened THE HOUSE OF CARDS, Card shop and Theatre booking agent. When he retired, the business was taken over by Derek Eagles in January 1987. The shop retained the same name and trade, closing in April 1991. GLASS of HONITON in June to November 1991. SIDMOUTH PET FOOD SUPPLIES 1992-1994. Next COUNTRY BLOOMERS until they moved to Fore Street in 1995. Another change of trade to THE NEEDLECRAFT EMPORIUM, advertised as the complete needlecraft specialist, closing in April 1999. Shop now called NUMBER-TEN.

Fortfield View.
   Mr. W. E. COLLIER. The family started the business in 1887, and in 1892 opened new premises, Undertakers, Joiner and Furniture Dealers. The Furniture business is still run by a descendant of the family, Noel Collier.

On the corner this building was The Retreat, a private house, Mr. Gibbs and family, 1889. Captain and Mrs. Warren, R.N. and Mr. R.M. Ellis, Professor of music in 1850. Later became The Sidmouth WAR MEMORIAL CLUB (founded 1922).

Harston.
   Apartments, 1919. Mr. and Mrs. Elizabeth Snell, 1922. In 1924, it became Michelmore, Davies, Bellamy, Solicitors, when they moved to here from Hope Cottage just across the road. Then to Hunt, Pomeroy, Michelmore. By the 1940s Michelmore, Davies and Bellamy. In March 2001, a merger with Michelmores of Cathedral Yard, Exeter, to be known as Michelmores, incorporating Michelmore, Davies and Bellamy. Mr. Richard Flack, managing partner.

At the top of the road facing down Church Street is Hope Cottage. The first business here were Solicitors. There was a Richard Rolle Drake and Steven and Lester Solicitors in 1836. We also have the names, Dark and Lester, with the date 1857. Next Lester and Radford in 1850. Also here in May 1863, The London and South West Bank, this was started here and remained until they moved to Fore Street in 1876. Radford and Williams, 1866. In 1877 it had become Mr. J. G. Radford, Solicitor and Mr. J. A. Orchard, Offices of the Local Board. By 1883 Radford and Orchard. Philip Michelmore, 1919, all Solicitors. Various Council

Offices, Urban Sanitary Authority in the mid 1890s. Board of Agriculture and Fisheries in 1902. Customs and Excise.

In 1925 Miss Radford gave Hope Cottage to the Local Board. In 1928 the Council moved all the Council Offices from the High Street to here. Later to move to Norton Garth in Station Road. The Devon County Library opened on Saturday November 7th. 1936. Another change for this building when it became, The Sidmouth Museum in 1970.

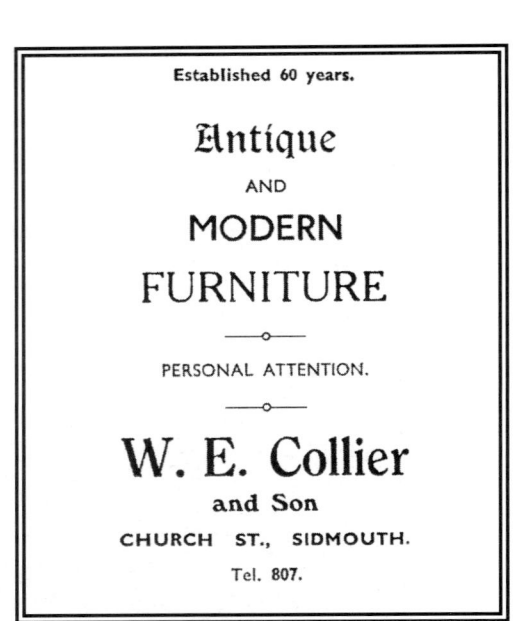

R. H. Spinks

Hair Stylist

PERMANENT WAVING — EUGENE
JAMAL — COLD PERM
TINTING — MARCEL WAVING
HIGH FREQUENCY

Opposite Parish Church Gate
CHURCH STREET
SIDMOUTH

Telephone 160

Established 60 years.

Antique
AND
MODERN
FURNITURE

PERSONAL ATTENTION.

W. E. Collier
and Son
CHURCH ST., SIDMOUTH.
Tel. 807.

James Lashbrook & Sons

LADIES' AND GENTLEMEN'S
PRACTICAL TAILORS

CHURCH STREET
SIDMOUTH
(OPPOSITE PARISH CHURCH)

SUITS TO MEASURE FROM £4-4s.
HAND MADE FROM £6-6d.

CHURCH STREET, NORTH SIDE

Frith Postcard

> **R. TANCOCK**
> Coach Builder & Postmaster,
> **Church Street, Sidmouth.**
>
> Post and Saddle Horses, and a large variety of first-class Carriages, constantly on Hire.

Sidmouth Observer and Directory — 1868

Starting on the corner by Church Lane. The first buildings were thatched houses or cottages, to Ebdons Court and became shops on the ground floor, in the late 1800s. For these we have the names; Robert Tancock, Coach Builder, Horse drawn vehicles 1857-1877. John Ebdon, Greengrocer, Builders, Undertakers 1821-1856. E. EBDON, Milliner 1836-1857. Chobey and Spencer, Antiques 1883. Henry Bartlett in 1877. W. Bartlett Bath Chairs, 1882-1895. Mary Tuck, Dressmaker, and Milliner. J. Spencer in the Market Place in 1856 and William Spencer, Horse Carriages, Donkey and Bath Chair proprietor here in 1878. Various members of the Spencer family here as Fishmongers, Greengrocers, 1893-1926. Mrs. Spencer. A. R. Baker, Honiton Lace. W. F. Conant, Fish Supplier 1889-1916. For the corner property, Mr. Chaplin, Watchmaker in 1926. Next door down, a reference for Vine Cottage, Antiques and The Old Curiosity Shop, Mrs. Sarah Eveleigh, Antiques and Removers, 1919-1927. The last property by the turning into Ebdons Court was the Baron Family. Mrs. Ann Baron, Lace maker and Greengrocer in 1866-1878, William Henry Greengrocers, Boot and Shoes 1885-1919, Percy Howard to 1926.

All these were burnt down in the big fire in 1927. The site was rebuilt in 1928-1929. Became Grenvilla House and Grosvenor Mansions as five flats on the first and second floors. The first floor also had offices. Grosvenor Mansions Estate office in 1935, and G, Bell, Chartered Accountant. Flat 1, Ware, Ward and Co. Accountants in 1939 - 1950s, also agents for the Halifax Building Society in 1945. The ground floor became three shops.

On the corner with Church Lane was The Electricity Showrooms opening in 1931. In 1935 as EAST DEVON ELECTRICITY Co. Closing in 1937 on moving to the High Street. WINKWORTH and LIBBIS, Antiques about 1939. NORMAN WINKWORTH in the 1940s. Cyril E. Huggett, THE ANTIQUE SHOP in 1951. Changed to a Toy Shop, Nursery Furniture, L. T. STAMP, 1958 to late 1960s. Next THE STABLE DOOR and in the early 1980s changed to THE SIDMOUTH FLORIST, who are still trading here.

The second shop down the road, Frobisher House, was, MARGUERITE, Dulford Nurseries to the mid 1930s. R. H. WITNEY, Grocer and Tea Dealer in 1936. They were also agents for The Devon General Bus Company. Change to HEALTH FOODS of SIDMOUTH in late 1950s. SOUTHERN HEALTH FOODS in 1969.

VITALITY HOUSE about 1981. Next LEADERS and to LIFECYCLE in 1987. Back again to SOUTHERN. These were all health food shops. Closed in March 2001. In September a new trade opened, P. S. MONOGRAMS, Embroidered Leisure and Workwear.

Second-hand Shop and A. R. Baker, Lace Maker

The third shop, Amyas JERMAN, Stationers to about 1935. TUCKERS, possibly a Shoe shop. Mary Tuck, Hat Shop, early 1940s. Cyril E. HUGGET, Antiques and Auctioneer 1946-1952. H. M. HAIG, Soft Furnishing to 1973. VANITY FAYRE in 1975.

G. HADLEY, Hairdresser. HAIR BY GEOFFERY about 1980. THE GROSVENOR HAIR SALON, October 1986, and now called THE GROSVENOR SALON.

Drake House.
  EVELYN M. BAILEY mid 1950s. Dresses, Corsetiere. ELEGANCE, Ladies Outfitters, in the 1980s. LITTLE CHARACTERS. Children's Clothes, April 1987 to September 1992. SCARLETTS, Fashion Boutique. Opened February 1993.

  Dormy House
We have a reference for Mr. James Jones, Watchmaker, 1902-1926, and Mr. Chaplin, Jeweller in 1927. This may not have been as a shop, as the lower end of the building was, Mr. Fred Hill, Restaurant Rooms in 1919. In 1921, COSY CAFÉ, which was here then offered for sale by auction. In 1930-1931 it was Tea-rooms, Mrs. E. Slinger. Then, THE PUFF SHOP. By 1935 it had became the DORMY CAFÉ, Mr. G. C. McLanghin. By 1939 Mrs. McLanghin, as THE WILLOW TREE CAFÉ. Later a change of owners who carried on as THE WILLOW TREE, Restaurant and café.

  Turning into Ebdons Court.
There was several small cottages in the mid 1850s. Traders, Henry Meryfill, Timber Dealer. Mary Wench and Ann Hurley, Lace Makers, Thomas Evans and William Weeks, Boot makers.

Grosvenor Cottage.
  Mr. Harris 1930-1940s, Primrose Cottage. Three Cottages in 1930-1940s Tuckers, Hatchley and Barnes. Spencer House, Mr. A. Mallon mid 1940s. alterations to one cottage for NORMAN MILLER, Chiropody, early 1950s to 1990 when it was made into Holiday Flats.

  Back in Church Street. On the corner is Ive Cottage. Private House.

Next down the road was a private house before it changed into a shop. The first name we have is Gallin and Brown, Hairdressers, who where here to 1927. We have not been able to find who was next here before Mrs. K. E. Coats, Confectioners, Tobacconist in 1935. In 1952, Mrs. Usher, THE CHOCOLATE BOX here for about three years. Mr. N. Tuxford, Sweet Shop. Mr. Reed also a Sweet Shop. The Sidmouth Herald used the shop for a display window for a very short time. Overmass & Chapple, in 1978. Next as Young Saffron, Boutique in 1979. In September 1981, John HOLLICK, Men's Hairdresser.

The next buildings to the corner with the Market Place, entrance in Church Street, the first reference for a trade here is for Mr. Robert Bartlett and his fourteen year old son Henry, Fish Shop in April 1826. Robert did the fishing from his own boats, Henry ran the shop. They were here until 1877 when they moved across the road. On the Market Place side was Theophilus Mortimore, Poultry shop 1883 to 1886.

The thatched cottages, were bought for demolition by the Local Board for £700. The Cottages were pulled down in 1886. In the Sidmouth Journal, it stated, 'That the walls were over four feet thick and needed strong men and horses for the demolition. In the centre of the block, large slabs of dun-coloured stone and other indications were found in an old chimney, thus showing that the building was erected between 1574 and 1587'.

Tenders were required for new dwellings and shops in December 1886. The road widened and the corner pavements were improved. The new building called SHEFFIELD HOUSE was built, and became GLIDDONS, Ironmongers. This is one of the oldest family run businesses in the town. The outside of the building has not changed, except the colour of the paint. Over the years the inside of the shop has been altered and enlarged. The shop had a wooden floor with counter facing the door, behind were row of shelves full of cardboard boxes. One could, like Sellek's in the High Street, buy any small number of things, not all prepacked in plastic, screws, nails and anything for household repairs. Mr. Gliddon seemed to always have to get out his old wooden steps to find the right box. The outside was hung with galvanised buckets, broom heads, garden tools etc. Over the years the inside of the shop has been altered and modernised. It is still run by the Gliddon family, as GLIDDONS, COOKWARE CENTRE.

ALL SAINTS ROAD

Back to the top of the High Street. We can turn into All Saints Road, which used to be called Mill Lane. There are a few small shops.

On the corner of the High Street next to the Unitarian Chapel, stood The White Hart Inn, which was built about 1710, and demolished in 1886. The last Licensee was Mr. Billy Sweet.

The demolition of the Inn enabled the entrance to All Saints Road to be widened. At the same time the Unitarian Chapel had a new porch and window built on the north side and a low wall and railings, Most of the railings have gone, probably for the war. However the low wall is still there.

Behind the Inn was a garden which was enclosed by a brick wall, and two houses, one of which was occupied by the Colwill family. On part of this site Jubilee Terrace was built. The road branches off to May Terrace and Blackmore View, private houses, one of these was Sidmouth's first Hospital, 'May Cottage'. At the end of this road is Church Path and The Victoria Cottage Hospital.

J. Ankins

Coronation Day 1937

Back into All Saints Road. On the corner is a shop, which is at the beginning of a row of 22 terraced houses going up the road. The first date and name which we have for number one is for 1883, Mr. James Colwill, Nurseryman, Greengrocer, in 1910, Colwill and Son, also Builders in 1914, and the same name running on into the mid 1960s. Then the property became EILEEN'S, Greengrocer by 1967. There was a change of trade to become THE COPPER KETTLE, Café in 1987 and next THE MUSTARD SEED Café, and Christian bookshop, opened in 1990.

On the North side of All Saints Road, past the side entrance to Sidlands House, there is an archway which led to an abattoir, Mr. Summers, Workshops and garages. Mr. Channings workshop and office. Emery's Motorcycle Specialists in the 1950s. Now all rebuilt.

We now come to the shops on this side of the road. The first one by the archway was a Butchers. The first reference we have as a shop is in 1910, Mr. James Summers, Butchers. By 1923, Mr. Oscar Summers, to the mid 1930s. Next it was Spurway and Sons, to about 1981. Another change to Malcolm Turner, all Butchers shops, closing in November 1989. Now the shop front taken out and is a private house.

A house which used to have the front door in the centre facing the road with a small front garden. The garden was built on to make a double fronted shop out to the pavement. This became The ROYAL DAIRY, Mr. J. Harris, Dairyman in 1889 to 1902. Mr. Harry Orford in 1935. Changing to Sidmouth Dairies by the 1940s. Then change of trade, to J. Hamblen, Lingerie in 1949. By 1951, Sidmouth Nurseries. T. R. Sellek and Son by 1952. Next change, C. R. CHANNING, Plumbers

By the 1960s the shop was made into two shops. the right hand side stayed as Channing's Plumbers. Then it became an Antique shop by 1981, Hilton's. Next, Mr. David Dory, Antiques and books in February 1988. In 1995, Devonshire House Antiques, having moved here from East Street. shop now called ANTIQUES CENTRE.

The new shop on the end opened with Mrs. Channing, as Eveyln, Ladies Hairdresser. It was then taken over by Mrs. Scott, still trading as a Hair Salon. In 1990, Mr. Geoffrey Ward, HAIR DESIGN. This closed down when he moved to The Littlecourt Hotel. In 1999 it was opened by Lisa Mortimore as TANGLES Hair Salon.

EAST STREET

We will now walk along East Street, the turning in from Fore Street. This used to be called Theatre Lane. On the north side, stands Caxton House, which is a shop on the Fore Street end. (See Fore Street) The back of which was the printing works. From the early 1800s most of all the local printing was done here, including the local paper etc. The printing press is now in the Museum. Then the premises became the Sidmouth Herald Office. Then alterations were made and a shop was formed, RIVA, Ladies Clothes, opened in 1997 trading until December 22nd. 2000. The shop was refitted and Val King opened in May 2001 as THE EXCHANGE, Ladies Fashion Agency.

Next door is a private house, before we come to what used to be the stables for The New Inn. The earliest date which we have found is 1807, with a reference for Henry Board, Groom and Hostler, who was there for 21 years. We also have a reference for the Lew Lakes Livery Stables. Later to be York stables and yard, with a coach house and hay lofts.

On Wednesday 10th December, 1879, at 7 o'clock in the evening a big fire broke out in the coach house. As it was thatched, the fire soon caught hold and reached the hay lofts. The west of England Fire Engine was directed by Mr. Blackmoor. A major difficulty was the lack of water, as it had to be carried in buckets by local people. The cottages between the yard and the printers on the corner with Fore Street caught fire, and the cottages near Mr. Bales and Mr. Whittons were threatened. The roof of the Globe, on the other side of the road, caught fire but was soon put out. The workers managed to put out the fire, before the Insurance Company's fire engine arrived from Exeter at 10.30.

The yard later changed to Trumps Yard for Trumps Stores in Fore Street. the right hand side sheds were storage of dry goods for the shop. The back row was stables, carts etc. on the left, sheds and garages. They had their own petrol pump for their vans and for sale. Most of it was burnt down in another fire on August 17th.1935, the garages, vans, bicycles, and petrol pump were lost. The fire was stopped before it reached Fore Street. Trumps rebuilt about ten garages and storage sheds. The council bought the yard in May 1958. The garages were let for various trades, Mortimore, shoe repairs, Bridgeman, upholsterer, P. Eley store room, K. Stone, upholsterer. All demolished in 1983, for rebuilding as Trumps Court, new flats for the elderly, in 1985.

The rest of the road comprises a private house and five cottages extending to York Street. From about 1926 to the late 1950s, number 5 was Mr. Charles Stone, Boot Repairer, not a shop.

On the other side of the road were small cottages, which mostly housed local trades people.

6.   This was used as the Festival Box Office 1996.

7.   Was a Theatre in 1803 - 1805, which did not succeed. This later became the Globe Inn. This was also the home of the Cuddy's Nest Jazz band, in about the mid 1930s. The Globe Inn closed in May 1938, when Mr. Vallance opened The Balfour Arms in Woolbrook.

The stables at the back of the cottages became a Youth Club, and for a short time it was called Kitchener's. Also at the back of the cottages was S. H. Mortimore, Boot and Shoe repairs, in 1925 and into the 1970s. The two cottages were demolished in 1998 to make car parking spaces.

The end cottages were altered and made into The Saddlers Arms, 1886. This was later to be part of the corner shop in Fore Street (see Fore Street). In July 1993 the first floor was opened as Devonshire House, Antiques, remaining there until 1995, when they moved to All Saints Road. The property is now part of Delderfields shop, with the entrance in Fore Street.

J. Ankins

Cottages demolished 1998

HOLMDALE

Mainly terraced houses on both sides of the road. On the north side of the road we have the name, John Teed, Blacksmith, 1897, by 1910 he was in the High Street. Samuel Daniell and Son also Blacksmith, 1897-1926. William Daniell 1930-1935. This was behind the shop which is now 72 on the High Street. Other names, Mr. J. G. Clarke, Sid Vale Iron Works in Holmdale in 1902 but not the location. This probably was after a Blacksmith forge or smithy which is on a early map, shown near the bottom end of the road.

On the South side is the back of Thatched House, now a shop in the High Street. On down the road was HOLMDALE GARAGE, Elliott Breach, was the founder and owner, 1919-1925. W. STAPLES, 1934. SPENCER'S, GARAGE, 1951 to about 1968. Sidmouth Motors in 1982. Auto Repair Services in 1988. Now converted into flats.

Part of Holmdale was called Stockers Court, at the lower end of the road, built about 1840, there were three cottages. The owner thought he was not getting sufficient rent money so he had a wall built right up through the middle of the cottages to make three into six. Three faced onto Holmdale and three onto the yard at the back. At some stage these were made into various small shops to the end of the road.

18. BUYERS and SELLERS, Furniture in about 1938 to mid 1940s. RAYLI, DIY. 1951. The Handyman Supplies to the mid 1970s. Holmdale Printers, Lithographic and Letterpress in the late 1980s. Mr. and Mrs. Tully.

18A. HOLMDALE Studios 1984

20A. Howe and Davis Ltd. Model Railways Engineers, 1952. P. White Turf Accountants in the 1960s. Next Mr. Ray Patch took over, a Picture framer and handyman. Mr. Patch sold the business to a gentleman who lived in Vera Cottage, this business was taken over by a Mr. Trowsdale and his son Timothy when the gentleman was unable to continue through ill health. Printing was the next trade to be carried out on these premises. Mr. and Mrs. Tully, put in two printing presses and various printing equipment into the garage. A photocopier and office in the shop with store room behind.

20. Ministry of Labour, National Service Office, Resettlement Advice Bureau, 1947/1951. OMEGA ELECTRICS, on the ground floor, they made electrical boards and fittings. Russell Ellis used it as a store for his electrical business after Omega. The first floor was let to Goviers China shop as a depository. The premises were bought by Mr. and Mrs. Tully who converted part of the building into living accommodation, with number 20A. On the ground floor was a large dining room, kitchen and small hallway with stairs to the first floor. On the first floor one room had a concrete floor with a trap door into the shop below, apparently this was part of the glove factory. Under the back garden there was a pit that had

been used in some part of the tanning process and also several very thick stone walls, and a very old sewerage system of slate and brick.

J. Ankins

1990, Corner Shop with Holmdale

14.   The corner site with Mill Street. In 1884 Mr. Sleep proposed to build a Glove Factory on land bought for £365. A two storey building was built. The roof had four large wooden vents on the ridge. They were there until 1998 when they were taken down and slated over. The Factory did not last long and the ground floor was then used for various trades. Mr. Elliott Breach, Practical mechanical motor engineer, in 1919, Mr. Arthur Jelly. Grocer in the 1923, HOLMDALE STORES. By 1947 TRIM'S STORES, Mr. and Mrs. Trim. In January 1949, the shop was bought by Mr. and Mrs. Taylor and they were here until 1963. The next reference we have is, The Elite Typing Agency in 1969. Pat Luxton and Mrs. Harris, ran the Typing Agency until it was taken over by Mr. and Mrs. Tully, as SOUTH WEST TYPESETTING in the mid 1980s.

In 1998 this corner shop was demolished and the site cleared. The remaining part of the building was converted into The Sidmouth Weight Training and Fitness Club. The official opening by Alderman Ted Pinney.

Telephone:
Sidmouth 765.

Telegrams:
Capt. P. White, Sidmouth.

Captain Percy White

Turf Accountant

THE COTTAGE, EAST STREET, SIDMOUTH.

———o———

Post, Phone or Wire your Commissions.
Accounts opened on approved References.

FURNITURE DEPOSITORIES

HOLMDALE, SIDMOUTH

(Opposite Grand Cinema)
Phone **993.**

Removals and Storage a Speciality

BEST PRICES GIVEN
FOR
High Class Secondhand Furniture and Antiques.

Reg. Proprietors :—
L. J. Huggett,   G. B. Carter   H. Peel.

MILL STREET

J. Ankins

1959, Mill Street

Turning in from the High Street, we reach the first building on the North side.

In 1837, Mr. W. Beavis, owner of the house and Blacksmiths Shop, he built the Wesleyan Chapel at a cost of £600. Sold to the Y M C A, and opened in January 1886.

Cottages 1 to 8. Numbers 1 and 2, thatched cottages taken down in March 1960. Rebuilt and opened as the Job Centre and Department of Employment. Number 5, was Sidmouth Council of Service in the mid 1960s. Mr. A. J. Sydenham, Boot and Shoe repairs, to 1980. Mr. Mortimore in 1983. Not shops.

9. This was a Garage, Mr. Woodley about 1876. Poole and Larcombe 1877. Bill Martin, 1937, Martin and Son, in 1940-1950s. Northcotts Mill Street Garage and later a Tool Hire Centre, until they closed in December 1989. Site cleared and the land is now a Council run car park for local residents.

J. Ankins

Northcotts Garage

For Your NEW or SECOND-HAND MOTOR CYCLE

CALL AND SEE

BILL MARTIN

(LATE OF B.S.A. MOTORS LTD. & MARTINS GARAGE)

THE RIDER AGENT.

Agent for All Leading Makes of

MOTOR - CYCLES and CYCLES.

ALL MOTOR & MOTOR-CYCLE REPAIRS
Undertaken and Carried Out on the Premises.

Mill Street Garage   -   SIDMOUTH

Tel.: Sidmouth 666.

10/12. Cottages to Holmdale. In 1937, R. J.Wilson, at number 11, Radio Services. In 1966, Numbers 10 and 11 were demolished.

14. The corner site (see Holmdale). We cross over Holmdale to the other side of the road towards the river.

15. On the corner Charles Maeer, Beer Retailer in 1878, The Dolphin Inn. Mr. Sleep built a new house on this site about 1885, called Merrifield House, which faces onto Mill Street. The manager of the Gas works lived here for several years. For many years there were two large metal hinge hooks in the wall on the side of the house, we were told that this carried a gate across the bottom of Holmdale Road. In 1995 The Red Cross bought the house and made it into their Sidmouth Red Cross HQ. In August 2001, Sidmouth Help Link and East Devon Citizens Advice Bureau moved into part of the building.

Next along the road towards the river was the Sidmouth Borough Parochial School built by the Feoffees and supported by various powers. The school was built facing a small yard. There were two stone porch entrances with gabled and slate roofs. One was for boys and one for the girls. There were 80 boys and girls. Headmaster was Thomas Canniford and the Headmistress was Miss D. Harding. About 1900 Mr. F. Drew, Headmaster. In 1914 the Headmaster was John W. Baldry, he said the Schoolmaster's house was too small and he refused to live there, so he lived in No. 1 Cambridge Terrace, Salcombe Road. Then the name was changed to The National School, into the 1920s. When the school closed it then became the Parish Hall and was used by the local boxing club, The Church Lads' Brigade, Mr. C. Colwill's Band of Hope, Saturday night dances. A general centre for families living around Eastern town. Then in 1947 the building became Potbury's Auction Rooms. The last Auction took place on 19th April, 1985. The building was later extensively altered and made into houses and renamed, Counters Court.

16. The school masters house.

17/18. This site was part exchanged for a site next to Potburys in the High Street, when Mr. Farrant wanted to enlarge his house during the 1840s. The Poor House was erected on this site. This edifice was a square, bleak looking building with two front doors set back from the road. It later became the Feoffees home. The ground floor was used for Offices, The National Deposit Friendly Society, late 1930s-1963. Sidmouth Consolidated Charities, in the mid 1960s.

The building became empty for many years until in April 1999 when it was demolished and the site cleared.

J. Ankins

17/18 Mill Street

    The end two cottages were a Police Station and Jail. The barred window can still be seen in the remains of the outside wall. In 1890 the building was a Fire Station, Harry Newton, captain. By 1910 it had moved to Church Street. The Police Station was moved to a terrace house in Newtown, which became The Constabulary Station, by 1890, having had a Prison cell built on at the back. The cottages were pulled down. Part of the end wall remains.

20.   The Mill, built in 1801, with mill stream or leat and water wheel. The mill leat was man made taking the water from the River Sid just upstream of the water fall in the first field of the Byes now called 'The Lawn' and rejoins the river under Number 24 Mill Street. First name we have is Merrifield Mills in 1890. Later the Mill and Forage Stores in the late 1890s, and then it was known as Sidmouth Mills in about 1894. Mr. J. Harris ran the mill, he was also agent for the Queen Insurance Co. In 1919-1935 it was run by Walter Harris. The premises were later to be called The Sid Dairy, under the name Mrs. W. Harris in 1939 into the 1950s. The Mill Leat was purchased by the S. U. D. C in June 1948, and was filled in 1950.

    We now reach the river and ford with the footbridge to Millford Road. Remaining in Mill Street, starting by the bridge there is a row of terraced houses, Numbers 22/30.

The first of which is Number 22. This was formerly a small shop, Mr. J. S. Endacott, Greengrocer in the mid 1930s. They lived next door at Number 23. In 1951, Mr. P. J. Coldricks, into the late 1960s. The shop then closed and the shop window was taken out and alterations undertaken to make it into a private house.

J. Ankins

1959 Mill Street

Further on down the road, past the turning for Riverside. A group of cottages built on a triangle of land were Numbers 34 and 36, 41 to 43. Number 36, Mr. A. J. Sydenham, Boot and Shoe repairs, not a shop, in the 1940/1950s. He later moved to Number 5. These houses have been demolished, and the area is now a car park.

Still in Mill Street on the corner with Russell Street. There is a pathway beside two shops numbers 37 and 38, which leads to a building which was for many years was a Bakery. In April 1939 it changed to the Sidmouth Women's Liberal Hall. It was later used for upholstery and store room, before being sold in 1983 and dedicated as the Jehovah's Witnesses, Kingdom Hall. Closed in 2001.

37. This shop must have been built in the early 1920s, opening as The Co-operative Society, with the shop next door as a Drapers, here until the mid 1930s. Later as Vanes, Antiques. To Dorothy Hartnell, antiques in the 1980s. Next it became the TILE and PINE SHOP.

J. Ankins

1983 Mill Street

C. Healey

1906, The opening of the Co-operative premises

Inside the Co-operative Store

The Co-operative Bakery

38.   The Sidmouth and District Co-operative Society, Ltd. Grocers and Bakers, opened on September 17th. 1906. Assembly Rooms, Mr. and Mrs. H. Scratchley, in the 1940s. Mr. C. E. Huggett in the 1950s. Tom Sawyer, Furniture. WOOLCOTTS second-hand furniture, late 1950s. Change to R. J. HOOKWAY and SON, Bookmaker, betting office. Later changing to FERN, Wool Shop to 1984. Then TILE and PINE opened in March 1985 with their shop next door.

Sidmouth Museum

38 Mill Street

40.   The Acme Household Services, 1940 - 1950s. Not a shop.

43/45. In about 1920-1940s, one of these was a small shop, Mr Bartram Baker, Greengrocer. Then Mr. Elliott, Sweets. The site was rebuilt as a block of flats.

J. Ankins

February 1991, Dean's Lock-up Garages and Workshop

Horse and Groom now town houses

RUSSELL STREET

Starting on the south corner with Fore Street, there are small cottages. After the cottages is the site of the former Eastern Garage, George W. Hodge, in 1919, their telephone Number was 33. Later called Hodge and Co. They were followed by R. Poole in the 1950s. Now it has become part of the Consumer Market. Behind the garage was a cottage and various small outbuildings, one of which was used as a Bottle Wash.

J. Ankins

October 1959, Roxburgh Cottage

Further down the road, there was an entrance to Caseley Yard, we also have a reference for Mitchell's Waggon and Carriers, who were probably here around 1870 - 1890. Later Venn Caseley, Wheelwright in 1897 and to T. Caseley to about 1937.

Next along the road, there were some stables, occupied by Lakes. This was later redeveloped and Roxburgh House was built. Set back from the entrance that had two tall stone topped brick pillars. This was later demolished and became a car park before being rebuilt as 17 Flats in 1963. This in turn was demolished in 1978, and cleared for a car park.

Lastly we come to The Horse and Groom Inn. This was another old Sidmouth Inn, which for many years was run by the Hellier family. This has also now been demolished, and rebuilt as town houses.

There were more shops around the town. These included. One in Lymebourne Avenue, also a garage and workshop, Arcot Road, Chapel Street, Bedford Square, Parratt's Fish and Chip Shop in Stanley Place (York Street) in the mid 1920s-1940s.

Many trades people traded from home, in sheds and outbuildings around the back streets. Bathing machines, boat and beach huts for hire, donkey carts, gigs and pony traps, bath and sedan chairs. Chimney sweeps, boot and shoe repairs, cycle dealers. On the sea front there were baths and cafés, coal and timber yards.

Now we are at the end of our walk around the trading part of town and we hope that you have enjoyed this gentle stroll with us through the past.

There are many more interesting past events and people who initiated them, including all the changes around Western and Eastern Town, the Marsh and the Ham, but that is another story for another day.

If you enjoy Sidmouth you may be interested in my other two books. Sidmouth, Victoria Cottage Hospital 1873-2000. and Sidmouth, The War Years 1939-1945.

Sidmouth Observer

V. Caseley,
WHEELWRIGHT,
BUILDER OF LIGHT SPRING VANS,
Wagons, Market Carts, Dog Carts,
and Agricultural Vehicles,
RUSSELL STREET, SIDMOUTH.
GOOD WORKMANSHIP.
MODERATE CHARGES.
REPAIRS NEATLY EXECUTED.

1897

REFERENCES

1. The Beauties of Sidmouth displayed. Butcher, Printed for J. Wallis. 1810.
2. Survey of Devon. Polwhele. 1610.
3. Survey of Devon. Risdon. Circa 17th century.
4. Beauties of England and Wales. Vol. 4. I Britton and E W Brayley. 1803.
5. Samuel Curwen. Journal and letters. 1776.
6. The Beauties of Sidmouth displayed. Butcher 1810.
7. Beauties of England and Wales. Vol. 4. I Britton and E W Brayley. 1803.
8. Samuel Curwen. 1776.
9. Sidmouth in old picture postcards. G Gibbens.
10. Guide, early 1900s. P.O. Hutchinson.
11. Survey of Devon. W. Polwhele. 1630.
12. Sid Vale Association, Newsletter 19.
13. Glimpse from the past. H. S. Daniell, Sidmouth Herald, 1981.
14. Harvey's Directory 1851.
15. Sidmouth in old picture postcards. G. Gibbens.
16. Glimpse from the past. H. S. Daniell, Sidmouth Herald, 1981
17. Sidmouth Herald 1981
18. Devonshire Association.
19. Sid Vale Association Newsletters 25 and 26. E. Whitton.

Acknowledgements and References

Directories: Billings, Whites, Kelly's, Pigot & Co.

Harvey's Sidmouth Directories, Lethaby's Directories.

S.V.A. Newsletters.

Devon Library Services, Westcountry Studies, Exeter.

Sidmouth Herald, Sidmouth Museum, Sidmouth Library.

Cover from Post Card by F. Frith & Co.

Mesdames. M. Baker S. Bartlett, Boyce, Carter, Coles, Marks, Mathieson, J. Ridley and M. Tucker,.

Mr. M. Davis, G. Eveleigh, L. Evis, L. Eaton, M. Gooding, C. Healey, R. Lane, D. Porter, D. Richards, K. Stone, R. Spurway

and the many Sidmouth people with their "did you know --- ?", or "have you got---?".

Special thanks to Alan and Pat Tully.

Other recent books on Sidmouth include:

Old Sidmouth	Reg Lane	1990
Life and Times in Sidmouth A Guide to the Blue Plaques	Julia Creeke	1992
Sidmouth A History	Sidmouth Museum	2000
Sidmouth Cottage Hospital 1873 - 2000	John Ankins	2000
Sidmouth, The War Years 1939 - 1945	John Ankins	2001